To Ena
love 'n' light
Alec xxx

STRANGE THINGS HAPPEN WHEN SOMEONE DIES

Strange Things Happen When Someone Dies

– By Alec Laidler

Published 2017 by Sazmick Books

Web: www.granddadbooks.com

British Library Cataloguing-in Publication Data.
A catalogue record for this book is available from the British Library.

ISBN: 978-0-9954554-9-8

Printed and bound in the UK using sustainable resources

STRANGE THINGS HAPPEN WHEN SOMEONE DIES

ALEC LAIDLER

OTHER TITLES BY ALEC LAIDLER

Granddad You Have A Message: Spiritual & Inspirational Writing

ISBN; 9780956610331

Granddad You Have A Message II: Through The Eyes Of A Child

ISBN; 9780983008665

Available to purchase from

www.granddadbooks.com & www.amazon.co.uk/com

Self-Publishing Your Book Made Easy!

Sazmick Books offer self-publishing and marketing services to authors of most genres. We help to fulfill your ambition of getting your work from typed or written manuscript, into a printed book or E-book with customisable add-ons.

Simple packages, Stunning books.

Chat with us and get your book on the road today!

www.sazmickbooks.com

For All Your Self-Publishing Needs

DEDICATIONS

Along with the many family and friends I have to thank for all their support I would like to take this opportunity to dedicate this book to a lady who has been a tremendous help to me over the last five years and although she is no longer physically with us, the universe I believe chose this lady to assist me on my spiritual journey, and she has certainly done that, so with all of my heart and love I can say thank you to my wife Pat for being with me every step of the way.

Also with the sudden passing of my friend Mac Goldie, who has helped me to design and produce the covers of Granddad book's. It would be unbecoming of me not to say thanks Mac you are a true life friend. This man will feature much more later on in the book.

CONTENTS

PREFACE

I suppose I've always known that there was more to us than our human existence. My first "experience" of knowing came when I was a young boy and had an out of body experience, quite frightening really to wake up and find yourself looking down on your body asleep in the bed. Well to be quite honest I was more frightened of what people might say or think so I told no one of my experience (well I was only eleven years old, it was 1957 and attitudes were different then).It was not till many years later that a friend was telling me that she had experienced levitation at a party, that I divulged my childhood experience to her.

When I was at school I sketched in ink a drawing of a man having an internal bleed, little did I know that some years later I would be that man. It was at a time in my life when through personal circumstance I was deeply depressed (the ending of a relationship can have many differing effects on you). During the early hours of this particular day I had been ill and so I took myself off to my doctors, who seemed to think I had a bad dose of flu he told me to go home and go to bed, the thought of spending the day at home did nothing for me so I went into work. At work I was very restless and couldn't bring myself to do any work, my business partner came into the office told me I looked dreadful, my face had changed to various colours and I was now a very deep shade of green. At lunch time we were outside the office when I felt a terrible pain and I collapsed onto the pavement. The butcher, whose shop is next door to my office carried me back into the office and immediately rang for an ambulance. In the meantime I felt a sudden surge inside me and I ran into the toilet where my insides erupted with blood going everywhere. My memory from this moment is vague, but afterwards I could remember everything that was said and done, the words of the medic saying "we have no pulse" and me responding in my unconscious state "you must have because I'm talking to you." I was told later that I had died and they had brought me back again. My one regret was I never got to thank them for saving me so I do that now, later that night I was taken to the operating theatre to find out what had happened to me. Once again during the operation I found myself stood next to the surgeon dealing with me, and I made a vow that if I got out of this situation I would change my life or I knew I wouldn't survive. (well I am still here).The surgeon later told me that during the operation my body had gone into shock and they thought they had lost me.

I don't know how you feel about angels, but I am a firm believer as was my mum. During Pat's illness she spent a lot of time in hospitals, it was during one of those occasions I was at home with no one else in the house, when I heard whistling all around me, I couldn't recognise the tune but at the time the television nor radio were on and I realised that they had come to help us. Sometime later Pat was given two months to live and so we asked her children to come to the house the following weekend. When we were all together we told them the sad news, I was stood by the kitchen sink facing the family and felt a hand being placed on my shoulder, no one was behind me and so once again I realised they were there for us. Since Pat's passing there have been numerous occasions when they have shared their presence with me.

Well and so to the book I hope you enjoy reading it and get some feeling to the love, belief, grief and all the ways we are affected by someone we know and love passing to spirit, and know that how we cope with it will shape our life's journey forever.

FOREWORD

I feel this book largely represents the emotions of grief and my journey from the dark into the light since my beautiful wife passed into spirit in May 2011. It has taken me from the depths of despair to the discovery of who I truly am and to finding an inner happiness I never thought possible that will be with me forever.

ABOUT THE AUTHOR

I come from a mining family and I lived in the North East of England. My family moved to the Midlands in 1962 settling in the Tamworth area. My early working years were spent in an engineering environment working for companies based in the Midlands, but actually spending most of the time working away from home. In 1971 I moved into financial services and have spent the rest of my working life doing that until that fateful day when the love of my life passed over into the world of spirit and I couldn't find a reason to go on doing it any more.

During my life I have experienced several 'out of body experiences' and have had two near death experiences. I have always believed in life after death and Angels, but nothing prepared me for the fateful day in May 2011 when my beloved Pat passed away after suffering breast cancer. This book has been made possible because of a huge rise in my conscious levels after her passing and an enormous amount of spiritual help from the lady herself for which I will be forever grateful.

INTRODUCTION

Having already written two inspirational books under the title of Granddad you have a Message I have decided that although this book is inspirational it is a different format to the others in as much as it is about me which I believe to be a good reason for it also to be titled Granddad you have a Message. I hope you enjoy the read and gain whatever hope, inspiration, love and healing that you may need at this time in your life.

Chapter 1

IS DEATH THE END, OR THE BEGINNING OF OUR RENEWAL?

On the Sunday 30th April 2011 I had a strong feeling that I should ask Pat's friend Yvonne if she wanted to visit her in the hospice, Yvonne and Pat had become good friends during her illness though I had only met her very briefly once before. Well I rang her and she said she would love to join me on my visit to the hospice the next day. On the Monday we met and went to the hospice, we talked generally about various things, very different I would say to on our journey home.

As we entered the room Pat's whole being appeared to be raised off the bed and surrounded by gold and white light. I stood there amazed at what I was seeing I honestly believed it was the connection between Pat and Yvonne that had formed over the previous months. I said to them "I don't understand what's going on but I will leave you two to get on and I will go and see the sister" and I left the room. The sister told me Pat had had a disturbed night, that she was bleeding internally and her time was drawing near. On our way home Yvonne asked me many questions about what I believed in and I told her I believed in the afterlife, regression and angels, she told me she had been regressed and had had several lives with her husband Paul also in them however not always as man and wife, she went on to say that if I wanted to be regressed she knew a lady who would do it and was trustworthy. I told her that I felt at this moment I would be too tense but would consider it later when I was calmer. As we arrived at her home she told me her husband Paul was a medium ,I didn't really know too much about that sort of thing but little did I know how much my life was about to change because of it.

I now realise sometime later that what I had witnessed that morning was Pat's soul beginning its ascent to heaven and nothing to do with Yvonne, though I will take this opportunity to thank Yvonne for the friendship she gave to Pat at a very critical time in her life. During the early evening the family were gathered in Pat's room chatting amongst themselves and I was sat talking with Pat I don't know exactly what happened but I sensed a change in her and felt something different had happened I said nothing and we carried on talking. After we had left we returned to the house and went for something to eat, then we returned home, it had been a long day and we all felt tired. We all went to our beds and I fell asleep straight away only to be woken up and told to get dressed we were needed at the hospice straight away Pat's condition had changed dramatically and her time had come. I must say we travelled to Lichfield in record time and remember saying to our driver "slow down if she finds us up there when she arrives she won't be very happy". As we entered the room Pat lay dying and all around her bed are the other children and their families and Pat is failing fast and gasping for breath, so sitting down next to her I took hold of her hand and began to reassure her that all was well and that her family were close by. At this moment Pat opened her eyes and looked at me as I told her that I loved her and that it was time for her to go, and she gently slipped away into the long sleep that awaits all of us. After a few moments the Staff Nurse who had been stood behind us came forward and confirmed my wife's passing. I stood up and walked into the corridor to collect my thoughts having been witness to the most beautiful experience. I then went back into the room and sat down by her on the opposite side of the bed, the family had now moved into a room next door to compose themselves. As I sat there I realised that Pat's hand had become wrapped around my thumb, how I don't know but it had, it was as if she was saying" don't go just yet I'm not ready", a very weird experience indeed. I joined the family who were standing together talking about what they had just witnessed. Someone noticed the pointers of the clock on the wall started to spin round at some considerable speed, we all stood open mouthed when they suddenly stopped at 12-20am the time of Pat's passing. At that moment the

Staff Nurse came into the room and seeing our reactions asked what was the matter , pointing to the clock she turned and said "oh that it resets itself every night" we all burst out with nervous laughter, a light hearted end to a very traumatic but special evening.

When I got home and went to bed "just let me know that you are okay and I will be alright" I muttered as I fell asleep. At 7-30am I woke and got dressed ready to start ringing family and friends with the sad news. My first call was to my sister who had been with us for most of the past few weeks but had to go back to Newcastle shortly before Pat went into the hospice. It was 7-55am when I dialled the number, the phone rang once and was picked up straight away, before I could say anything my sister said "she's passed hasn't she" and I concurred, her words that followed gave me hope and a great deal of peace." I know because she has just been here, standing in jeans a top with her lovely blonde hair looking so absolutely radiant and as the phone rang she disappeared". This news I must say lifted the spirits of the whole family when they heard. My friends to me this is the beginning of a truly remarkable story one of unconditional love and the beginnings of spiritual awareness. Can I say at this point if there is one person on earth who I would believe beyond all others it's my sister she is as honest as the day is long and totally straight in what she says and does, Pat knew this she knew I would listen to her.

The next few weeks leading up to the funeral passed in a haze of running around doing the things that have to be done at this time. The family all returned to their homes and I continued in my own way to grieve for my loss. On their return for the funeral it was very noticeable how they had all began to pull together in a loving caring way. Let me say briefly explain there had been many petty jealousy's between them in the past, one thinking that one might have had more than the other which I would say wasn't the case, no one got more than another. I hope they will forgive me mentioning this, but I feel it is important what happened at this time be known. Pat wasn't a religious however she was a Christian and believed in God, but not the afterlife. We held a Humanist funeral for her, which was very personal and emotional. The church was absolutely over flowing with people who had come to show her their respect. I had not realised till then how loved she was by

3

so many people for so many different reasons. During the service two young ladies stood before us and told us how they would remember Pat and the impact she had made on their lives, of course what they didn't know was the impact they had made on her life and so I thank you both Natasha and Joely.

Natasha's Poem.

Words cannot express exactly how this feels, but what memories I have like your party at the Peel.
And lengthy afternoon chats over many cups of tea, about nothing in particular, or mostly family.
In the short time that I knew you, your inspiration was immense.
Your feisty nature and attitude, your bravery and your strength.
There are always many things that are left unsaid and done
Like how proud I was to have known you and to have married your eldest son.
But although you're no longer with us your spirit still lives on,
Not just in wonderful memories but in the lives of everyone.
Thank you Natasha for your kind words, you were so brave standing up in front of all those people and you showed great personal strength on that day. xxx

Joely's Poem

How proud I am to have known you Pat. Your laughter was so true.
Such an inspiring woman, I hope I could be like you.
You were dealt an unfair hand in life, but you accepted it with all your pride,
you never stopped smiling right up to the day that you died.
Every time I saw your face it brightened up my day
Just to see how well you coped in my mind your smile will always stay.
And those memories you gave us all will stay firmly in our minds.
The only thing we could have wished was to have more time.
You are at peace now Pat, no more fighting for you.
Lay your head up on that cloud, time to rest now.

God bless you.

Thank you Joely you were so brave standing up in front of all those people and of course you and Kelli were an immense inspiration to Pat. xxx

I also realised for the first time of all the help she had given to so many people. All in all a fitting end to a lovely lady or so you might think.

Chapter 2

AND SO LIFE GOES ON

Over the next few weeks strange things started to happen, the smell of flowers in the bedroom at different times of the day and night. The car would fill up with the smell of flowers while I was driving it. One night as I opened the front door a voice called out my name, "Al". I turned around expecting to see my youngest step daughter Sue but there was no one there, few people call me Al most use Alec. It was certainly a strange feeling.

My grief and depression seemed to deepen at this time and I tried to hide my true feelings from the family after all they had their own loss to come to terms with, I felt that these happenings were signs from Pat to show me she was still with me trying to comfort me.

Going back in time to nine years previously, Pat fell pregnant, not planned and being perfectly honest not particularly wanted so I suppose it was not surprising when she had a miscarriage. A life lost is always harrowing and sad and neither of us spoke too much about this to anyone, not even each other. I suppose we both felt that we had been punished by God for not wanting the gift he had bestowed on us. The reason I mention this episode in our lives is because one night when I visited a friend's house who happens to be a very spiritual lady gifted in mediumship, suddenly said to me "you do know Pat has a son in heaven with her, he must be about nine or ten years old". I was speechless as far as I was aware no one had been told of our loss and at the time this lady had not been in our lives, I smiled and carried on with the conversation. When I was leaving the lady gave me a present. She said it was her most treasured possession, but had been told she was to give it to me, the gift a cut glass prism, I asked what I had to do with it, she replied "you will know what to do with it" When I got home I held it in my right hand the prism became full of beautiful colours, purple, blue, green, gold and pink. These are the colours of my energy and this present was to prove so inspirational later on as I developed my writing and internet connections because it became the recognisable sign of Granddad Books.

However when the different things happened as stated earlier I found myself ringing Yvonne to discuss them with her. A few months after Pat's passing a friend of my family, John died with his funeral being held in Birmingham. None of my family wanted to go for various reasons and so I went though I felt it might be a bit of an ordeal. On the day I turned up at the Great Barr Crematorium and met up with the family many of which I had not seen for many years. The service started in much the same way as any other and the vicar asked us to say a pray for John and I lowered my head, to my amazement I found myself in pure white light, a trillion lit candles would not have shone brighter. It was awesome, pure and so serene. I looked all around there were no floors, ceilings, walls, windows or doors nothing except beautiful light and there was my wife Pat and stood alongside her was her dad (who had passed many years before). I must say I was shocked and didn't understand how this could happen, it was hard to believe. I looked up and the service was going on with the vicar talking, I put my head down, and was once again in the white light with my wife. When I eventually lifted my head I had a great big smile on my face Happiness could not describe how I felt, totally elated. I knew in this moment my wife and I would be together, forever bound by unconditional love for all eternity. Much later I was told that I had visited the halfway house where mortals can visit those that have passed over. As I stood up I changed my expression after all this was John's funeral and his family were obviously upset, it didn't seem right that I should be happy. With the service over I expressed my feeling with the family and left. When I eventually got into my car to drive home, the inside of the car filled with the smell of flowers and I knew I had experienced something few people had, Heaven on Earth, people at one with the Spirit World and so I thanked Pat for being there with me. The whole thing seemed so surreal but it certainly cheered me up. When I got home I rang Yvonne and told her what had happened, she listened quietly and I got the feeling that she wasn't surprised.

On another occasion I was visiting a friend who was going through a bad time as her fiancée had left her only weeks before the wedding. As we were chatting a vision appeared before me of an elderly lady in her dining room setting the table for a meal, the main feature in the room was a beautiful welsh dresser made of a very dark wood. As I began to tell my friend what I was seeing she recognised what I was describing as her Nan's dining room and the lady I described as her Nan. Her Nan was telling her that no matter what she would always be there with her, supporting her. As we walked out of the lounge I noticed a photograph on the side board I asked who the lady was in the photo she replied her mum and I said the likeness between her mum and her Nan was uncanny and she agreed.

Time moves on the family seem to be coping ok or maybe they were protecting me from how they truly felt. I did feel however that Pat's youngest was really suffering but I was not sure how or even if I at this time was capable of helping him. My depression at this time was getting deeper, at this point I was very desperate crying myself to sleep every night and waking up crying every morning, I might well have harmed myself and I made a decision to ask for help from the St Giles Hospice drop in centre which was located quite near my home. They arranged for me to see a counsellor the following week. A local charity had been really helpful to Pat and the family and the family decided we should donate some funds to them, so I rang Yvonne who was connected to them and asked if I could go around to her house with the donation. Little did I know that this visit would change my life forever.

Bereavement and Spiritual Renewal.

The sense of loss, the pain, the hurt, the despair and the feelings of total abandonment, all of these senses are felt on the passing of someone who was loved and cherished. Understand, none of these things would be possible without love, and the stronger those feelings are the more love there was. And so with the end of earthly life is the beginning or renewal of spiritual life, for their work here is done. And so it is not out of order for us to rejoice knowing that a loved one has been rejuvenated after their toil of earthly existence. And so out renewal must also go on without them for our work is not yet done, for our cycle has not gone fully round, as it must for all of us to achieve what we came to earth to do. For have no doubt none of us can return home until we have fulfilled our destiny. And when we do and we also cross over, then and only then will our loved ones and those who love and cherish us, will they go through all of these emotions of loss, pain, hurt, despair and abandonment as our ancestors before us.

For this is the way.

- Taken from Granddad you have a Message

Chapter 3

FOLLOWING A SPIRITUAL PATH

I rang the doorbell which was answered by the lovely Yvonne she then introduced me to her husband Paul. To be honest I don't know what I'd expected but he was nothing like I had imagined him to be. We had coffee and sat down talking about Pat and how I had been coping since her passing. I started talking about the youngest son, Dean and how worried I was about him. He out of all the other children seemed to be suffering most regarding the loss of his mum. Although he enjoyed a drink he seemed to be drinking more than he would normally, his whole demeanour had taken a bad turning for the worse and at this time I did not know how to help him. The conversation had moved on to a discussion on angels and how if you asked them for help they would oblige you, but you have to ask they cannot interfere without being asked. Paul at this point said "don't worry about Dean there is an older lady coming to help him that she had a partner and she would help sort him out. For some reason I couldn't not believe what Paul was saying and I must admit a certain amount of calmness came over me.

After a few moments Paul asked if I could see a peacock feather on the floor near to him, I told him that I couldn't, he then said "no it's not a feather it's a gold broach of a woman's head and torso with the bodice enamelled in blue and green, she was wearing the type of hat that would have sported a peacock's feather. He said it had just been handed down. I recognised the broach as one I had bought my mum many years previously and it passed down to us as Pat had chosen the broach when my mum had passed away along with other pieces of jewellery. I realised later that I had given the broach to my sister so that she could hand it down to my daughter and so Paul's words were even more accurate.

We carried on talking when Paul suddenly jumped up saying there was lots of confusion in the room and it was me who was causing it, that around me was loads of guilt and it was stopping me from seeing what lay in front of me. Now I know what the guilt was about and I had carried it for many years. This isn't the time to talk about it, but had to do with a wife who had passed away many years ago. He went on to say if I could get rid of the guilt I would see many wonderful things ahead of me, But I had to get rid of the guilt. "How" I asked and Yvonne told me to go home and write everything on paper to then go outside and say to the universe that I forgave myself and then to set fire to the paper, this I did and my friends I felt the most enormous weight fall off my shoulders. That night I went to bed and I didn't cry nor the next morning, in fact from that day on I have not cried in that way again.

The next day I called on Paul and Yvonne and told them what had happened the night before, Yvonne responded by saying that spiritualists and mediums would give their right arm (so to speak) to be able to walk in white light and thought that I was a powerful being. Let me say at this time in my life I certainly didn't feel it. Paul told me he held meetings on spiritualism on a Wednesday morning and suggested I might like to join his group, on the basis if I didn't like it I wouldn't go again. Can I say it has been important for me to relate this meeting with Paul and Yvonne because it was to be the start of the spiritual journey that I am now on.

The Golden Age.

Is it your birth or you're passing that matters? No it's your life in between. For you were sent here for a reason, a purpose, to enlighten your soul and the souls of others. And if we all do what tasks we were given, then the whole earth will be enlightened and the bright light will shine throughout the universe for every being to see, and we will be in THE GOLDEN AGE.

- *Taken from Granddad you have a message.*

Grieving and Healing.

On the Thursday I made my first visit to St Giles Hospice Drop In Centre for my appointment with the Bereavement Counsellor, she was very nice and I felt obliged to say to her that since my meeting with Paul and Yvonne my thinking and beliefs had changed and I was concerned that I might be wasting her time. Her reaction was very kind she told me that she knew of Paul and Yvonne and understood how he would help me. She went on to say that Pat was all around me and in fact I found this very comforting. However there were many stages to grieving that had to be addressed and she felt the counselling would still be beneficial to me and so the first of six sessions began. The first session involved me talking about my feelings regarding Pat's passing, meditation which I found very calming and visualisation which was not so successful but an important experience never the less, during this session she told me she thought I was someone special as I had orbs dancing all around my head and she felt Pat was very close to me The session ended and I agreed another meeting which was fixed for the following week.

Well my friends life goes on and my step daughter's wedding loomed closer. Although the chances of Pat being at the wedding had always been non -existent it was with some anticipation that I prepared to go to the big day "on my own" so to speak. For although the family and lots of friends would be there my Pat wouldn't and at one point I did have thoughts of not going at all especially to the reception, which was being held at a hotel only a few miles from where I live. The day arrived toward the end of July and the weather turned out beautiful and sunny. The marriage service went very well, with a few poignant moments when the congregation were reminded of Pat. By the end of the ceremony I felt more relaxed and began to enjoy the day and I must say the bride and groom looked radiant and happy which let's face it, this was their day the day all their dreams come true. At this point the photographs were taken in the church grounds and I made sure a picture of Pat was held by me on every occasion, to me it meant she was there. The reception followed more or less the usual things that you would expect, dinner, speeches, wedding gifts and of course the wine flowed, well, all good things must come to an end and at one o'clock in the morning I found myself alone in the hotel foyer, so I made my way to the room booked for me. Once inside I'm afraid to say I broke down and cried, asking my beloved Pat why she had to leave me and so I suppose the grieving process took another turn to one of anger. Next morning I awoke packed my bag and went home, vowing "I wouldn't ever go to another occasion on my own" and to this day I have not.

There are five stages of Grief and these are:-Shock/Disbelief, Denial, Anger, Depression and Acceptance. Some who are going through or have gone through grieving may suggest there is more. But this is my account. Firstly may I say that the stages do not necessarily happen in the order as they occur.
So here we go.

Shock and Disbelief starts when you are told that your beloved wife has only two months to live. The shock from this statement is immense and very painful, but from it comes a strength from within that says there is no way that we wouldn't fight this thing together not only for us but for the kids.

The second part of this is when you sit by her bedside after she has finally passed over and you realise that she has after all that fight and courage and your love one is no more, It is very hard to come to terms with the fact that someone who can fight like that with such tenacity, faith, belief and still not succeed.

Anger comes at your daughter's wedding, when you have gone through a beautiful occasion holding a small picture of your wife (so she would be there) listening to everyone talking, laughing and enjoying themselves, they all seem to be couples. The coming to the end of the evening and everyone has gone to bed and there is you on your own in a hotel bedroom and you cry and shout to her why? Why? are you not here, why have you left me what did I do wrong? And then you fall asleep, crying, on your own. I woke the next morning still feeling distraught, packed my bag and drove home to the comfort I found there.

Depression; my God you don't even realise how depressed you are trying to protect the kid's from your feelings, bottling everything inside, pretending to the outside world that you are fine and coping. The reality is you are going to sleep each night crying and you wake up crying feeling alone and abandoned. This is a dangerous time, thoughts of self- harm are in the mind, but the spirit within you gives you the will to go on.

Acceptance even though I have walked through a spiritual gateway and experienced some very loving and emotional moments with my wife, son and other family members who have passed, I feel humble that I have been able to do this, whereas lots of other people have to struggle through this nightmare without the comfort of knowing. I can never accept that she has gone because of the love.

Thank you for taking the time to read this, if you are going through this horrible period in your life I hope this will bring some comfort to you knowing that you are not alone and in fact over a period of time it does get easier.

My first spiritual meeting certainly went differently to what I had expected, and yet I shouldn't have been surprised as I really didn't know what to expect. When I arrived formal introductions were made to the four ladies and one man and we sat around in a circle. Paul talked about the previous meeting and then moved on. Everyone had a pen and notepad book for making notes but not me. In fact, it would be six months on before I used one, but that's something I will talk about later.

Paul began by saying that there was lots of energy in the room. Both ours and the spiritual and wanted us to see if we could connect to others to the other side, using meditation. And so we sat there meditating, let me say at this point I had no idea what I was doing and that would very soon become apparent.

One of the ladies was a visitor from America and Paul soon started to describe a lady and a situation that he could see, the following are not his exact words, but near enough for you to get the general idea.

He began to say that he could see a lady in the American South with three children. Her husband had died very early in their marriage, while the children were quite young, she made a living by digging for gold. It was at this point, the American lady said that she was almost sure this lady with her grandmother and one of the children would be her mother. Paul went on to say that she was being helped by a black lady from the area. At this moment appeared in front of me a black lady who appeared larger than life, dressed in beautiful coloured clothes, yellows, turquoise and red. Let me say, to me this was very unexpected and I immediately stood up and left the room, walking into the conservatory where I sat down I must say, somewhat in a state of shock. A Jamaican lady by the name of Josie asked if I was alright. I responded by telling her that I hadn't understood, she asked if it was my first visit I concurred and she told me not to think about it but to accept that this was the sort of thing for me to expect what I didn't understand was did this lady come to me or did I go to her. In fact, and I realised that she came to me and of course it is not possible for me to go to her that any of you have not been to a spiritual meeting this sort. I hope to have given you a reasonable account of the meeting carried on and eventually finished. I discussed the events with Paul and he simply said that I would experience many similar things in the future. The one thing that was sure in my mind was, I would definitely be going again. The door had opened and I had passed through and I was not going to be turning back to stop. After this I began to be visited by the spirit world on a very regular basis, both day and night. These visits, included meeting my mum and dad, my granddad, both my grandmother's, uncles, aunts, brother-in-law's and various friends who were also passed over. Some nights I hardly slept because of the volume of spirits, let me say this still goes on to this day, but not at the same volume of people, but it is very satisfying to know that my past family still love and care for me as they did when they were here.

!! Memories!!

Recalling the people we have met on our journey. The places we have visited the footprint we have created as we pass along the way. Moments in time, lessons learned. Remembering family, mothers, fathers, sisters, brothers and other relatives and friends, who in turn remember us, a gallery of thoughts and pictures to remind us of who we are and what we have become. Forever forged as one and an everlasting reminder, that we are one, interlocked and entwined together through time, the link with the past to the present.

11/04/2012 at 07-00 hrs.

- Taken from Granddad you have a Message.

My next counselling session went in much the same way as the first discussions, meditation and visualisation. I did however mention about my spiritual visits, which were occurring every night, my councillor was of the opinion that it was too much for me at this time and that I needed time to grieve. In truth, I agreed with her. I was certainly fascinated by it all, but I did need more sleep and so I asked to be left alone so that I could go through the grieving process. I must say I was blessed by the way she consoled and looked after me, but of course this is part of the training she would have gone through that said all the training in the world doesn't teach someone empathy and this lady had an abundance of it thankfully.

At the next spiritual meeting we discussed the point of whether we were all connected as a group and so we decided to experiment and see what the result would be. Once again we sat around in a circle and began to meditate. After some time of seeing and feeling nothing except the calmness, I began to see colours beautiful gold and purple swirling all through my mind, then a Native American in full ceremonial dress appeared in front of me and to my side was a Middle Eastern lady, all in black with her face covered, this time I was more prepared than my first experience and I just let everything happen. At the end of the meditation, Paul asked everyone about their experience, starting with me and so I began to relate what I had seen the colours, the Native American and of course the Middle Eastern lady. Paul responded by saying that all around my head and shoulders was the most beautiful gold and purple colours and that he too had seen the Native American another lady confirmed she too could see the colours and had also seen the Native American as well, I was quite astounded three of seven people had experienced a very similar experience, and this showed me that nearly 50% of us were connected.

That night I called round to Paul's and had coffee, I had taken into going to see him more often as each day seem to bring something new. As we talked, Paul said that Pat was with us, dressed in jeans, a top and looking radiant. She told him that he was the last person she had expected to talk to since passing, this I could believe because she certainly had not believed in the afterlife. This event certainly had a good effect on me, knowing that she was okay. On my way home my thoughts drifted over what had happened. I'm thinking, he's been doing this for 30 years and I wondered how long it would be before I had a similar experience, after all I had only been doing this for a matter of a few months. Anyway, I put the thoughts out of my head and proceeded to drive home. Little did I know what was about to happen. I had gone to bed and read for a while before switching off the light in no time at all I saw my lovely wife was running towards me laughing, crying and totally overjoyed. My feelings and emotions were the same the pure joy at seeing her and feeling her as she ran in my arms, my friends, I cannot give my feeling credit at this event only to say both of us were overcome and we cried. Was it a dream I asked myself, but I knew I hadn't fallen asleep. The whole thing was so surreal. The next day I went straight round to Paul's and discussed the whole thing with him ending by telling him I would never doubt my gifts again.

I had at this time begun to read and study quantum physics and healing. At one of my counselling meetings I was given the loan of a book titled "The Field" by Lynne Mac Taggart. It was about a series of chapters written about various people who had discovered for the want of a better word, the Zero Point Energy Field. A field of energy that is all around us invisible as fresh air, so to speak, but nevertheless very real. This energy field is only appertaining to the earth, no other planet. It was discovered by scientists during the Cold War and because the space race was given precedence, the Field was shelved and didn't emerge for quite a few years. It is not my intention to go into great depth at this moment in time. Suffice to say for spiritualists, it's a must read. My interest in healing was developing and I read various books on, Colour Healing, Crystal Healing and Spiritual Healing. At the end of my counselling, I had an assessment meeting to see how I was progressing and it was mentioned to me about a Reiki course that was about to start at the centre. Now I had heard of Reiki, but knew nothing about it and so I agreed to join the class. Firstly, to learn what it was, secondary to see if I could do it and thirdly to see if I was any good at it. This decision has proved well worthwhile. There are many people who have the knowledge and skills to use Reiki for healing and many books on what it is and how it should be used. My own feeling, that it is universal energy given by God to be used for the healing of the body and mind for the greatest good and the greater good, and to be giving with love. The energy passes through the practitioner's hands to the person receiving the healing. They may be affected in many ways, feeling the warmth and seeing colours and sometimes they may see the spirit of a loved one, let me say this is not always the case and does not happen to everyone. But the general feeling of peace, calm and well-being would be experienced by most people. If you want to experience Reiki or feel you would like to become a practitioner find a healing centre or Holistic group and join a course.

And so, as ever Christmas time comes around. I usually visit the north-east of England to see family who live up there usually I stay with my sister and generally speaking have a good time. One morning as I layed in my bed and found myself in darkness surrounded by stars, my being seemed to be taken into outer space. When I turned and observe the earth in the distance and a voice told me that I was not an Earth Being, but a Cosmic Being with that I was once more in the bed. My friends this happening truly astounded me, not in a frightening way, but in an awesome way. I know I should have been scared to death, but actually I was very calm and at peace with myself. A truly remarkable feeling. I realise of course that this was something called astral travel and made possible by my conscious levels at that time. The rest of my time in the north-east was quiet and uneventful and I returned home to spend Christmas holiday with all the family. The first Christmas since Pat's passing. There were no meetings over the Christmas period and it was not until the middle of January, before I recalled the happening in the north-east. Once again, Paul didn't seem to be surprised so I decided I would like to do more of this astral travelling and I asked the universe to help me. A few weeks later, Paul was reading spiritual message to us when he said that one of the group and asked for help with astral travel, I was gobsmacked as I had not told anyone of my request and so he was not to know, the reading went on to say that help was being sent and when I left the meeting it was with great anticipation. As I said earlier astral travel is a state of consciousness and over the next month I made journeys over the Alps, the Mediterranean and outer space. Once again I had been given another spiritual lesson and my apprenticeship for the want of a better word, continued.

Consciousness.

It's what level of consciousness you are at that will determine your place in universal existence. The lower your level of consciousness the longer it will take for you to achieve your aims in life. Your ability to love unconditionally, to feel empathy, to understand yourself or other fellow beings is all determined by the level of consciousness that you have. To increase your level of consciousness, which we all must do would enable you to do all the things that at this moment for you is not possible. Travel throughout the universe, visit planets and zones that you don't even realise are there, mix and join in with peoples from other zones and existences. All of these things we have always been able to do, but through ageless time have forgotten and let our level of consciousness drop to the lowest levels. And now is the time to increase that level to face the New World with all its challenges.

For this is the way.

GOD's way.

- Taken from Granddad you have a Message.

During this time I was experiencing various dreams, one of which was a vision of a beautiful young woman, WOW I can remember thinking what did she die from, thinking she was a spirit but a voice told me she wasn't a spirit she was a human like me and they were sending her to help me with my spiritual journey. I do not remember dreams very often but I have never forgotten that woman. I am mentioning this event now because a few months later she appeared again once more I thought she was an angel until she kissed me full on the lips.

This kiss was so powerful it sent energy throughout my whole body an amazing experience all I could think was blimey I didn't know angels were supposed to kiss like this. My friend I relay this to you now but later in the book you will find out what a powerful affect this young woman is to have on my life.

In another dream I was in a vast room full of spirits and I was addressing them from a platform which also had other spirits on it, this appeared to me to be some sort of meeting but in truth I did not understand what was going on. At a much later time on a Saturday Mary Magdalene told me she had been to a Light warriors meeting that she attended every Friday night and she was surprised not to see me there. I was wondering why she would expect me to be at a meeting with her when she lived thousands of miles away from me, it was then that I realised this meeting had been within our conscious levels. I told her that I didn't believe I had been to any such meetings, she told me that generally we don't remember the meetings. I mentioned to her about the dream I had months previous about the room full of spirits and she thought that this in fact had been a Light warrior meeting. Well my friend it seemed that once again a vision/dream that I had had was ratified as happening within my consciousness, strange indeed.

Chapter 4

I SEE TROUBLE AHEAD

Just when you feel that there is light at the end of the tunnel, well my friends we have all heard of the saying and we all know it's not always what it seems to be, and so it was that morning when Pat appeared before me, giving me a warning to some troubles that were about to happen. I must say in the back of my mind I had half expected it but hoped it wasn't going to happen.

When Pat passed away I gave the four children some money, one part they were to have straight away and do with as they please, the second part was to be used for their future benefit as and when required a leg up, so to speak. Well, the problem was Michelle the oldest daughter wanted her money now and as this wasn't what Pat and I had agreed, I told her no. The conversations went on for a few weeks without resolving the situation and then Michelle stopped me seeing my grandchildren rightly or wrongly, she thought this would make me change my mind. Unfortunately I saw it as blackmail and I was not prepared to give in and so we reached a stalemate. This was to go on for quite a lot of months.

It was during this time that I paid a visit to one of the pubs in Birmingham that we used regularly when I was working in Bourneville. As I walked into the pub one of the bar staff told me she needed to talk urgently with me and so we walked outside. Let me explain a few months earlier she had heard me talking about some of the strange things that was happening to me and she told me that both her and her mum believed in the Angels, that they were both sensitive to things. Well, having gone outside she told me that she had seen Pat, who was wearing blue jeans and white top her hair in a bob and wearing red shoes, she had a warning of trouble for me. I thanked her and explained that Pat has already warned me. The interesting thing was that the girl had only ever seen Pat twice in the pub and both times she had no hair due to the chemo so I was surprised by a description of Pat came with her hair in a bob I thanked her and went back to my colleagues in the pub. At the next meeting I was recalling to the group the day at the pub and talking about the girl's description of Pat's clothes in particular the red shoes. At this point Paul said Pats with us now and she is laughing regarding the shoes. She was saying ask Al about my shoes. Well, Pat's shoes had been a standing joke for a long time, when I first met she was showing me around her home, reaching her bedroom and looking in, I could see lots of shoes on shelving to one side of a chimney breast and lots of handbags on the other. There was 100 pairs of shoes marked 1 to 100 and corresponding matching handbags so number 50 shoes went with number 50 handbags, I thought it was hilarious couldn't stop laughing. This was what she was relating to once again the spirit world had shown me that they are as of today, as the present moment.

A few nights later Pat introduced me to my son, Pat had miscarried some years before (I mentioned this early in the book), stood before me was a boy with beautiful brown eyes. I asked what his name was, she responded Philip, and I was not surprised as he had being looked after by Pat's dad, who had called his son Philip, so why wouldn't he name this boy the same. After all, he was his grandson, and let me say Philip continues to visit me to this day. The next day I was sat in the lounge feeling upset, when I sensed Pat's arms around my shoulders comforting me, my friends, this was a very emotional moment and one I won't forget.

It was around this time that two very important things in my life happened, the first I started to write down all the inspirational things that came into my head and though this is going on now for many months. I didn't realise how important it was going to be to me in the future but we will talk later about this, the second thing was to do with meditation and let me say at this point I found meditating to say the least difficult and so after discussions with Paul, it was decided that I would go to a local Buddhist Centre to experience how the Buddhists went about it so to speak. So one Thursday morning, Paul, Yvonne and I turned up at the centre to take part in a lesson and to meditate. The teachers were very nice and helpful and having duly signed in we were shown to the temple which was situated at the top of the garden. Sitting down towards the back of the room we were lead into a meditation by one of the teachers as I sat there I looked up at the teacher and next to her on the stage was a gentleman wearing a dark grey suit, he seemed to be looking at me and smiling. It was quite a shock to me when I realised it was the spirit of a friend of mine Arthur who had passed over some years before he seemed pleased to see me and the feeling was mutual. Pat appeared standing with my mum and I must say this really amazed me and made me very happy at the same time. In fact, during the meditation session a whole array of family spirits came to me, when we finished the meditation I told Paul about my experiences, he told me to tell them that I was there to learn more about meditation and that they should leave me to do that. We went several times together and I went quite a lot of times on my own. The lessons on inner peace and love were a great help to me with the grieving process I was going through and my meditation skills improved tremendously. I bought a CD to further help me with meditating and still use it to this day. In fact over the next few months I bought quite a lot of them, and presented them to the people who came to me for healing as it helped them to relax prior to the healing. Meditation is a perfect way to help bring peace, calm and harmony into your life, especially in times of stress, grief or for whatever is causing some disarray in your mind. My friends take an hour out of your day and try it, at the least it will give you a bit of quiet from your daily routine, at best peace of mind, tranquillity and finding out who you really are. If you find it difficult to meditate like I did try a local Buddhist Centre. It will certainly help.

Who is Philip?

Who is Philip? he is an auburn haired boy with beautiful brown eyes.
He is 11 years old.
He was brought up by his granddad, who named him after his son.
He lived with his granddad till his mum arrived to look after him.

He is a cheeky boy, with a great sense of humour and love for football. So you might be forgiven for thinking, he's just like any other boy of his age.

Well, yes, but Philip is different, he is the result of a pregnancy which ended in a miscarriage all those years ago.

He lives in the land of spirits, who is he? He is my son, always loved and never forgotten.

For this is the way

- (This is a page from 'Granddad you have a Message Book 2: Through the eyes of a child')

During the early afternoon, I was sat in the lounge, I looked towards the television and a white mist seemed to appear in front of it, strange I thought that as I looked my granddaughter Mini appeared lying on her tummy in front of the TV with her head cradled in her hands. As I watched Pat appeared standing next to me, and we watched Mini together. After what seemed an age, yet probably a few minutes they both disappeared, I will say right now. I was confused. After all, Mini is alive and well and so I couldn't quite make out how this event had occurred. The tingling feeling stopped and everything returned to normal. The next day I was attending a spiritual meeting in Birmingham with the Wednesday group. During the interval I took the opportunity to discuss the previous day's appearances with Sandra a member of the group. Let me say Sandra is a very powerful medium, having told her everything, and also my concerns about Mini. She told me that both Pat and Philip were trying to tell me something concerning me and the family regarding Mini she asked if Mini was sensitive to spirituality. I said I thought she was as when we lived in the previous house she had told me there was an old man sat at the bottom of the bed, he was my friend and he had passed away in that room a few years earlier, she didn't know that. In another house we lived in for few months while we were waiting to move into the present house she told me she had seen a lady on the landing I asked what she was wearing, she replied a frock so I was pretty sure Mini was very sensitive. My friend told me that she felt Mini was missing me as much as I missed her and our two energies had joined together, the rest of Saturday went without any further occurrences. On Sunday morning I woke up to find both Pat and Philip at the side of the bed. She was stood and Philip was standing on his head. I asked her what he was doing and with this he swung himself upright and they both started laughing. They were playing a joke on me and obviously found it very funny. Let me say I had already worked out the spirit world are very much up-to-date with our lives and what we do. I find this very comforting and hope that you will too. Anyhow, I think you would agree a strange and wonderful weekend. A few weeks later I was at Pat's previous husband's house and mini was there, it was very upsetting her mum told her not to speak or have anything to do with me. Knowing how we felt about each other this was very hard for the both of us. I tried to reassure her everything would get sorted in the end, and then I left. In the car, driving home I cried and cried. This was one of my deepest moments of despair, but I still wouldn't give in to my daughters demands and I suppose my ego made meeting her demands all the more difficult. Even though other family members, particularly Sue the youngest daughter talked with me on numerous occasions, but I couldn't see past myself, if you can understand my meaning. Well, a time I had been dreading was upon me. The first anniversary of Pat's passing, as with all families in this position. There are always those moments, or occasions that are going to happen. As I lay in my bed that morning Pat came to see me, typically to reassure me and the family that she was okay. I wrote a little piece that morning and I would like to share it with you.

Remembering Pat

Today we remember lady who passed by 12 months ago. A kind person, who never failed to help anyone in need a wife, mother, grandmother and a friend to many, and as she passes by, in a little black dress with a tear in her eye, Un-noticed by everyone. Well, almost everyone.

Love.

- (A page from Granddad you have a Message. Book 1).

It just caught my mood at that moment in time.
That afternoon I sat in a chair in the lounge and I felt her put her arms

around my shoulders and comfort me. You may be forgiven for perhaps thinking that the emotion of the day had had an effect on me. All I can say to you I truly felt her and the love from her and it certainly helped.

At this time I feel that I would like to talk to you about healing or healers to be more precise. I have mentioned earlier that I did not have a lot of time for mediumship; this is something that I have had a change of heart about. Let me explain to you why.

Firstly, I was invited to go and see a medium at work, where he was doing his skills at a hotel in Solihull, West Midlands. There were approximately 200 people in the audience and we are all paid what I would consider a reasonable entrance free to being there. This was the first time I had been to one of these nights and so I waited with a certain amount of excitement for him to start. Throughout the evening several spirits came through him to various people in the audience, some people were happy to have been picked out some anxious but generally speaking, most were more than pleased. The reason this evening was so special came about with about half an hour to go to the end of the night when he picked up the vibration of a young man who had passed recently to spirit and wanted to give a message to his wife who was in the audience, now this lady was sat with her friends two rows back from me and to be quite honest, she was in a very upset state of mind, couldn't come to terms with her husband's death, and actually I don't believe she wanted to, in her own words she wanted to die and join her husband. The medium talked to her and her friends for nearly an hour explaining how close husband was to her all the time, how he was concerned for her welfare because of our badly she had took his passing. The lady began to calm, the medium asked if she wanted him to carry on. She said yes, yes this was what she had needed and what she had come for. In ordinary time this meeting would have finished long before it did but the medium would have none of it and carried on talking to her for quite a while longer. The message here is she came because she needed to hear from her husband, he came through for her, the medium was able to comfort her and the healing process had begun for her. She may not have gone home totally healed, but she went home with the knowledge that her husband was okay, on the other side and so a healing process had begun. At this point I will reveal to you the medium's name Steven Holbrook and if you get the opportunity to see him work, please do.

I suppose it is natural to think a medium would use all of the skills, seeing, sensing and feeling. This is not always the case as it was when I went to see a medium called Julie in Harbourne , which is a suburb of Birmingham, she could only feel things.

This visit came about when a friend Jackie and her two daughters invited me to join them to see Julie. It was agreed between us that nothing would be said about me or my abilities and we met at Jackie's aunt's house. Both of the two girls talked with her and then Jackie, this lasted for about two hours and then it was my turn. As I walked into the room she asked if I was interested in classical music, I said I might be and she told me she could hear vibrant music, as if she was in Vienna. I must admit I am a great Andre Rieu fan and go to many of his concerts, so she was pretty accurate. Without me saying anything else she asked who Ann Marie was and I asked if the person had passed over or was still this side of life she confirmed the latter and I told her it was my sister. The mention of Lavender was next and I confirmed since Pat's passing this was a regular scent in the house.

She told me she could feel the presence of a lady who felt hot all over and kept asking "what are we going to do now Al what are we going to do now". Of course I recognised my wife PAT and the day we found out she only had two months to live. We got home from the hospital and we stood in the hall and held each other closely and those were the words she kept repeating. There were other things I recognised and some I didn't, but she told me all would become clear in the fullness of time. She talked about two people Joyce and Joe, the lady who was unwell but kept it secret and the man who should have passed three times. The lady Joyce was a client of mine for many years and we became friends. There came a time when she was really unwell and I asked her if she wanted to tell me something. Her response knocked me for six so to speak, she told me she had cancer and that it was terminal, but she did not want her husband to know at that time and made me promise to keep her secret. Of course I did. The man Joe was the dad of my best friend when I was growing up and I was privileged to be looked on as one of their family, over a period of years Joe had three massive heart attacks and it was the third one that he didn't survive. Another thing she asked if I had cats in my house, I told her no but three cats regularly pass through my garden and still do to this day, there were other things she told me, some I understood and others I didn't, but she said all would be revealed in the fullness of time.

She had asked me at the beginning to hold a pack of Tarot cards and now she wanted me to choose six cards and hand them to her. This I did, firstly she was amazed as I had chosen the six top cards including the death card, but she assured me not to worry as it was in the past. As for the rest she told me I was going to have the most amazing life and then she asked me who I was. I told her of all the things that were happening to me and the gifts that I was discovering I had. She was astounded and told me she couldn't do any of the things except feel things around her. We finished with her asking me to keep in touch with her and I agreed I would.

At this time I was experiencing many different types of visions, sometimes people, sometimes video like pictures of the past and I suppose also of future events.

One such vision was of a rather beautiful woman and I asked them upstairs what she had died from. Their reply was that she was not a spirit but a human and they were sending her to me to help with my spiritual journey. A few months later I had another vision of her and we kissed full on the lips, I am not over exaggerating when I tell you every part of my body went POW and my thought was I didn't think angels were supposed kiss like that. I have related this to you now but later on in the book it will take on a fantastic new meaning, but for now we will leave this here for now. Other visions have been regarding babies and all of the predictions have come true, except one but I know in the fullness of time that will also come true. I know that once I see something I cannot undo it or take it back.

Sometimes the visions are of the past, one such vision was a meeting of the war cabinet during the Second World War it involved Churchill, Eisenhower, and De Gaul, I was at that meeting. This was followed by me in full flying kit climbing into a Lancaster bomber and settling into the front gunner's seat. After a while we were in the dark flying over I think Germany when we were lit up by lights and flashes of light and lots noise and then a huge loud bang and everything went black. The next thing I knew was my granddaughter shaking me and telling me to wake up. I concede it may have all just been a dream, but the man I was named after was killed in a Lancaster bomber just before the end of the war.

This brings me nicely on to an experience I have had recently in the Yorkshire Dales. It all started with me taking a colleague who is a financial adviser to see a client of mine who lives in a farm house on the out skirts of a small village near the town of Richmond which origins date back to Viking times. Having introduced them we all sat down in the lounge, they sat on a window seat at one end of the room and I sat at the opposite end of the room listening to them discussing her finances. I became aware of a tall very dark haired man with a large beard standing next to me, watching the other two. He wore brown leather riding boots, trousers, a lace frilled shirt and black jacket, to give you a better impression he was like someone out of Pickwick Papers. He just stood there for quite some time and then disappeared. I didn't say anything to the others at the time, after all this lady lived there by herself. During this visit I also sensed someone in one of the bedrooms and also sensed a cat brush past my legs and although the lady kept cats they were not any in the room at that time. I did tell my colleague about the happenings as we were driving home.

My next visit to the farm occurred about six months later. I think at this time I should point out one or two things which you will see the relevance of as we go on. The village dates back to the Viking times and in the seventeenth century the farm was a working Creamery and had milking cows there. The family who owned the farm had built a much bigger house and moved into it. Part of the farm house was turned into a flat with access off a lane running along the side of it.

In the spiritual group I attend a friend and I discussed an article in a spiritual magazine that suggested a town in Co. Durham was the spiritual centre of the North East of England and so we decided to take some time to investigate. I rang the lady in Yorkshire who ran a B&B at the farm and booked an overnight stay for the two of us. Because the lady had been a client of mine for many years she would not accept payment for our stay, so we took her for an evening meal at a local hotel. When we got back to the farmhouse we had coffee and my friend Colin went to bed. As the two of us sat talking about the years we had known each other I noticed a lady stood looking out of the window. She wore a long dress and her hair at the back hung very low and was tied with a bow about half way down. I didn't say anything, I just watched, she stood for a while looking out at the view of the Dales and I must admit they are stunning, and then she disappeared. We talked for a while longer then I went to my bed. As I entered the room I could sense the smell the cows and all the other smells of the farm, now I found this very strange as it had not been a working farm for a very long time, in fact for over two centuries. Well I undressed and climbed into bed and turned over looking toward the window.

After a short time I began to get the feeling that I was being watched and so I turned over to look toward the other wall, to my astonishment there stood the man I had met on my previous visit and next to him the lady I had seen earlier that evening. He was dressed in boots, riding trousers and a white shirt, she was now dressed in a long linen night dress and her hair hung loosely down her back. They turned to leave and I asked them not to go, he turned to me and I enquired what his name was, he replied John Williams and then they had gone. The next morning at breakfast I asked Colin if he had slept well, he replied that for the first time in many years he saw his mum who had passed over some years before. I then relayed to him my experiences and he asked if I was going to say anything to our landlady. Before I answer she walked in carrying the toast and asked me point blank had I seen anything, so I had to tell her and she gave me some history about the farmhouse and I agreed to do some research. Many months later she told me another Medium staying there had seen a small boy. So it seems a family from the 1600s are still living there as they did all those years ago.

My research suggests that John Williams was possibly to do with a copper mine that was working at that time and by his dress sense I would say he was probably the manager and they had lived in the flat at the farm whilst he worked at the mine. I would suggest by his appearance and name that he was a Welshman. Using the internet I was unable to establish any record of his birth in the area.

What I believe is that the spirit world exist on a parallel zone to us and I just wonder, who did they think I was sleeping in what could have been their bedroom.

It was a Friday morning the next visit from Pat happened and it brought to an end the long running saga of me not seeing my grandchildren because of the disagreement with my eldest step daughter. My wife stood by my chair and told me that Michelle would never be able to buy a house so wouldn't need the money as a deposit and so I should give her the money as I needed to see the grandchildren and they needed to see me and after all she said Michelle will only spend the money on the kids and with that she disappeared. In the post that morning came a letter from Michelle saying exactly the same thing as Pat had said and so I rang her and told her to come over to me and we would sort everything out. She arrived a few hours later and brought my granddaughter Mini with her a joyous occasion, that evening she brought my grandson to see me and so a very angry unsavoury part of our lives came to an end. Thank God. However I do believe that if I had listened to what Pat and Philip had been trying to tell over the previous months this situation would have been resolved much earlier. But as I have said previously I am new to all of this and still have lots to learn.

As we come to the end of 2012 it is worth mentioning and talking about the Mayan Calendar. The Mayans along with the Aztecs were on the earth many thousands of years ago, although proof of their existence is still visible throughout the earth. They were very advanced in the way they lived compared to other parts of the earth and it makes you think they had outside help. The Mayan Calendar ran for five thousand years at a time and December 2012 was deemed to be the end of that calendar, of course some people including some of the media went with the fear that the world as we know it would come to an end. This of course proved to be totally wrong and what we spiritualists believed it was the end of one level of consciousness and the raising to another. The Golden Age of Enlightenment. This is something that wouldn't happen in one day, but over a period of time. This is going on as I write.

The consciousness of our world needs to rise considerably as the earth at this present time is not in a good place, racism, hatred and ego are at the forefront leaving love, empathy and forgiveness way behind and this needs to change.

Chapter 5

MY SPIRITUAL JOURNEY CONTINUES

Well my friends first of all let me just say spirituality cannot be taught it is already within you, it is a case of looking deep inside yourself and finding your soul your inner being. Whenever you have a problem ask your inner being it will never lie to you, it may not tell you what you want to hear but at least it will be the truth. Up to now I have talked in the main about the spirit world Pat, Philip and so on, so let us look at the broader picture.

I don't know about you but I know very little about Quantum physics, basically the air we breathe is an energy field and the earth is the only planet with it. This energy field is unique we are not part of it, we are it. Each one of us is an individual piece of that energy and each one of us creates our own reality, positively or negatively whatever our choice is. So actually there should be no reason for hatred, racism or revenge because we are all one and it is only these egoistic, power seeking people who have divided us through racism religion and differing financial structures on the basis of divide and rule.

The energy field is called the Unified Energy Field and was proven to exist by the Accelerator which is based in Switzerland during Christmas 2013.At this time I channelled "your scientist have been allowed to make a very important discovery but they do not understand what exactly they have found". In fact the field is not just energy but consciousness itself, love, empathy and forgiveness but also greed, anger and ego, as the Golden Age develops we will see good take over from the bad things that hold the earth back today.

Within the field there are various zones Elementals (inner earth), Earth, Spirit world, Angelic Zone and the Cosmos as Universal energy comes into and blends with the Field it pushes all of the zones closer and closer together, therefore a raising of your conscious levels is inevitable and will bring the spirit world closer to us and within the reach of far more of us and the need for mediums will not be so necessary for us to see and talk with family and friends who have passed over.

The Field, God or Man?

What makes us tick? ....We do.
What makes us ill? ....We do.
What makes us better? ....We do.
What makes us remember? ....We do.
What makes us emotional? ....We do.
What makes us care? ....We do.

The list goes on and on, and the true answer is the Field.
The Field you might ask. What Field?
The answer: "THE ZERO POINT ENERGY FIELD ".
The energy that surrounds us unseen every day,
But only now is it being recognised as not only being, existing, but for what it actually is, an energy so powerful that stores information, that creates and cures illness It's been there since the beginning of time, that feels emotion, that constitutes every possible thing and situation we find ourselves in. It is the creator. But most of all it is us , for we do not exist in the Field, We are the Field, therefore we are the creators of our very existence and through us and our consciousness we can reach out into the universe and into different worlds. For we are far more than we pertain to be, we are universal beings.

For this is the way.

Well my friends as with anything in life, change happens when you least expect it, as it was with the next part of this story. As I recall it was afternoon in June when I began to feel the need to write and so I picked up my pen and pad and the words began to flow, for probably fifteen minutes and then I finished writing as quickly as it had started so I closed the pad. Within a few minutes I needed to write again a continuation of the last piece I thought, but no this was a totally different, to be honest this was unusual and to date this had not happened before well I finished and put the pad down.

At the spiritual meeting the next day Paul said it would be different as he had written two pieces, both being totally different and so I listened with interest to what he had to say. When he had finished and the group had discussed the content and meaning of the readings, I showed Paul what I had written the previous day and though the words were different the meanings were the same. Paul began to read other writings I had done in the pad (let me say until then I had shown no one my writing), he was amazed and told me I needed to get the writing out into the wider world I replied that I was writing a book, his reply was not fast enough and left it at that.

Well that night the Universe told me to use modern technology, to replace my old computer and get onto the internet. This would be a completely new experience though I used a computer during the course of my job I had had no interest or experience of using the internet. Well the next day I went shopping and bought everything I would need to move forward. I started by doing something I would never have thought of doing, I went onto Facebook as a place to post my writings on and then I started a private group called 'Granddad you have a Message', this proved to be a whole new pathway on my spiritual journey. The group would be a stepping stone for people who are just staring on their journey and also for people who are in the varying stages of theirs. Any new members to come from likeminded people whom I invited to join, who read and showed interest in my posts on Facebook.

One of these people was a lady called Sarah and her husband Mick who were self-publishers of their own books. I decided to contact them and ask for information on how to go about it (with this book in mind). We arranged a visit for them to come to my home and to look at what I had written. Well Mick read the journal or at least as far as I had got, while Sarah sat reading all the messages I had channelled. After some time had passed Mick told me that he loved what I had written and to get a move on with the book, easier said than done, because writing this book was taking a lot out of me emotionally and I was finding it quite an ordeal. On the other hand Sarah thought my writings were special and unique, she told me that with them I already had a book and we should publish it. By the end of that afternoon it was decided to go ahead with the book of channelled writings with a launch date in December 2013 and so the race was on to get it sorted.

I never realised the amount of work involved, the technical aspects and so forth. Firstly we set up a website www.granddadyouhaveamessage.com, then a Twitter page with the same name and all of my posts on Facebook went directly onto Twitter and very slowly I began to get followers from all over the world, all of these things to be used to build up my profile on the internet.

We had several meetings over the following months as the book began to emerge from all of our ideas. I wanted the book to be small enough to fit into a coat pocket or a ladies handbag. There was to be several coloured pictures in the book and the artwork for the cover was sorted out. I decided the title would be 'Granddad you have a Message' as it seemed a logical thing to do as all the other things came under the same heading, which at this point let me explain how this came about. When my granddaughter Mini was three she put a message on my mobile phone so that every time I had a message I would hear her voice saying "Granddad you have a message" and so I used this with everything connected with the book. Another thing that I decided to do would be to give all the profits from the book to two local charities, the first Breast Friends who are a group of local ladies who devote their time and effort to helping other ladies who have or have breast cancer, this also includes helping their families. At this point I would like to once again thank them for all of the help they gave to our family during Pat's illness and even after she had passed away, they will never be forgotten. The second charity The Kelli Smith Appeal, again a local charity to which through my long standing friendship with the family I felt the need to help raise the funds for Kelli who has a childhood cancer and may need to go to USA for treatments which at the moment are not available in the United Kingdom. The target of the fund is £500,000 and I am sure with the drive of her mom and step dad Tom plus the rest of the family and friends they will surely achieve their goal.

Well by the end of November the book was finished and a date was set for the launch in my home town. The local press took an interest and helped promote the book and I invited a number of family friends and colleagues to join me in the launch and partake in a Cheese and Wine evening, which would take place in a local bistro on the 17th of December 2013. On the night the room was full of anticipation about the book and after a few words from Mick and myself "Granddad you have a Message" was launched. During the evening Mini and I sat signing books for the people who had bought , music played in the back ground and the cheese and wine was enjoyed by everyone, a good night.

Then of course the real work began of actually marketing and selling the books. Well Christmas was then upon us and everything eased off for the holiday, well not quite everything because Mick had arranged for me to do an interview about the book on radio, so on the afternoon of 23rd December I found myself talking to a guy called Paul Giovanni of Critical Mass Radio. The original idea was to record the show as I had no previous experience but after a long chat Paul decided he would like the show to go out live and so at 8pm that night I made my radio debut. My publishing friends came over and supported me and amazingly my dad who had passed over many years previous stood in the corner of the room, I felt he was also supporting me. Let me say at this point I am a fairly shy person when it comes to talking about myself but Paul put me totally at ease and we talked about the book and all things concerning the book and also the spiritual effect Pat's passing had had on me spiritually up to that date, many of the things which I have already told you about which was very difficult for me. In truth I found it enjoyable, but also a great way to advertise me and the book and so it was decided I would have to get over my shyness and do more radio work.

Over the next few months my life was taken over selling books and various radio shows here in the UK and in America, which I must say was good fun and very enjoyable. Another thing I was concentrating on was building up my profile obviously the radio interviews helped tremendously, but I was also trying to do the same using the internet on Facebook, Twitter and my own website. My main concern was developing the Twitter site and six months after the book was launched I only had thirty two followers and this worried me, it seemed to be very slow and I began to panic a bit. I asked various people what I might be doing wrong and what I could do to put it right, but although they used twitter no one seemed to be able to help me. You may well recall the host of Critical Mass Radio Paul Giovanni, well at the time of my first interview he did say if I needed any help to contact him and so I did. I told him what I was trying to achieve with my Twitter account, his advice was stop trying to run and try walking in other words slow down you're doing ok but you're asking too much of yourself. I must say this was sound advice. He went on to say he would introduce me to a friend who lived in Arizona, that he would have a chat to her and ask her to contact me. Her name on Skype is Mary Magdalene, my friends little did I know at the time but this would be a life changing moment for me.

Before I proceed let me for a moment tell you about some happenings and visions I had which will I hope help you to understand or at least follow where this story is going. One morning I wrote an inspirational piece and at the bottom I doodled a formation of what I perceived to be stars, now not being someone interested in astrology I asked one of the Wednesday group what she thought they represented and straight away without hesitation she replied Pleiades "The Seven Sistars." I must confess till this moment I had never heard of them. Then I was contacted through twitter by a Pleiadian Group and I also began to receive what I can only describe as messages in my dreams regarding Pleiades.

Well Mary Magdalene contacted me and we began a long discussion, firstly she asked if I knew where she came from. Without hesitation I replied Pleiades, I don't know why but I just knew and I also recognised her as the woman in my visions which I had seen months earlier. We carried on talking and she told me she was in contact with my wife Pat and began to tell me things that there was no way she could possibly have known. She talked of a red hat and tea. Well when Pat had her chemo her hair fell out and although she had chosen hair piece to wear she decided to wear a red hat instead and was lovingly known within the hospital as Pat the Hat. Regarding the tea I thought she meant that because I didn't like tea Pat would make me a cup and tell me it was coffee, but Mary Magdalene didn't think it was this Pat was going on about. I then remembered in the two months before she passed away we went to see a Chinese Dr who had given Pat a concoction of herbs and spices to drink every day as a tea, it was vile but I insisted she drank it. After a chemo session Pat's tongue would go green and furry, the tea cleared her tongue and after a few days her tongue would be pink again so it was obviously cleansing her blood. Mary Magdalene then went on to mention my son in spirit, she told me he forgave me for he knew I didn't want us to have a baby but he also said he loved me and would be waiting with his mum when my time came to join them. Again this was another fact Mary Magdalene could not possibly have known about but all these things gave this lady a lot of credibility in my mind. This first conversation ended after three hours, with us agreeing to talk again the next day. That night I decided in my next conversation I would talk to her about my visions of her and that kiss (which I still remember vividly).

Well the next day we made contact again and I asked if I could make one or two observations about what I had experienced in the past, she agreed and so I told her about my seeing her in a vision months before and I asked if she had seen me at the same time, she replied no she had been told just three months previously that she would be coming into contact with me and she was to help me all she could.

I then told her about that kiss; my friends she fell about laughing for quite a while before saying to me that we had both had many lives previously and that the two of us had been brothers, sisters, parents and man and wife before so the love that had transcended hundreds of years was bound to have had a profound effect on me. She then asked me if I had sported a beard in 2013, I replied I had, and I told her I would send a photograph. Mary Magdalene then went on to say in that year she had been struck by lightning and had woken up in a room of pure white light no floors or ceilings (I believed this because I also have been in that room in 2013). Well she said she saw people walking toward and acknowledging her. Included in these was a man in a long robe sporting a beard. That evening I sent her a photo, she Skyped me straight back to confirm I was the man in the room of light. My spiritual journey was beginning to go much deeper than I had ever imagined it would. Now I am being told I have (or my soul) has been around for thousands of years, that I originate from Pleiades and in fact I was one of the first to visit this planet and that Mary Magdalene and I have had many connections over many years.

During this conversation Mary Magdalene told me that she is a mum to two boys and she lives near to Tucson in Arizona, that she hosted a radio programme on Love and Light Radio and that she wanted me to do some radio with her so I agreed. We did several shows in the second half of 2014 with me, my website and my Granddad book being extensively advertised both by Mary Magdalene and the radio station website. In return I supported the programme by providing the finance for servers and also helped as a co-host on Mary Magdalene's shows, this has proved immensely helpful to me in raising my profile and making people all over the world aware of me Alec Laidler the author. As a consequence of this my Twitter following has rose dramatically along with my Face book friends. All of this was to enable me to reach out to a far greater audience with my messages. At this time I also began writing articles on Internet based spiritual website, purely to reach out to more like minded people.

For many months I had suffered severe pain in my lower back it was so bad I could only sit down for short periods of time. Eventually I went to see my GP, after examining me he told me the solution to my problem would be to have back surgery. This surgery involved removal of part of my lower spine and would leave a rather large hole which would have to be packed every day for three months by a nurse. As I live on my own I just couldn't see a way that I could have the surgery, the alternative was to take pain killing tablets every day and so I opted to do that and started to take eight tablets every day.

Every year I try to go to Maastricht in Lindberg (Holland) to watch a live concert performed by Andre Rieu and The Johann Strauss Orchestra.

Well I set off from Birmingham airport and flew to Amsterdam, from their coaches took us to Eindhoven where we stayed overnight. The next day we were taken by coach to Maastricht, in total this involve over six hours of travelling which I had to stand for most of the time because of the pain and of course I had to stand throughout the concert, you may well think why put yourself through that pain well my friends if you get the opportunity go and see this man in concert the whole thing is played outside in the main square and is absolutely magical. Of course after the event I had to repeat the return journey home and suffer the pain again.

Well I continued suffering for several months until one night I just had enough, when I went to bed I asked the universe for help as the whole thing had become unbearable and then I went to sleep, I began dreaming? And found myself in a field overlooking a valley, thinking how beautiful it was. In a while a craft appeared hovering just in front of me at the front there was a big entrance covered by what appeared to be a black mesh. As I looked I felt myself being drawn into the craft I made no attempt to resist and allowed myself to be taken inside. Amazingly the only thing I could see was brilliant white light, very warm and two pair of translucent teardrop shaped blue eyes and I felt hands wrapping around my body and the most wonderful feeling of being loved. This seemed to go on for quite a while and then I woke up in my bed. Ok you might say I had a dream, well I cannot deny that or otherwise but what I do know was that I had felt tremendous love and the pain in my back was healed. Over twelve months have passed and to this day I have not taken any pain killing tablets, I might also add I have just arrived back from Maastricht and undertook the whole week end with no pain and the concert was to me even better than ever. Was it a dream, I don't know but whatever happened it has had an enormous effect on me and my lifestyle.

There have been various visions/ dreams over the past few years and I believe them to represent past lives. Various dreams have been from biblical times where I have suffocated twice in earth quakes when I have sought refuge in buildings. The one dream that stands out is of an ancient scholar teaching me whilst I sat at his feet. In more recent times I have dreamt of dying in two different car crashes, also of walking down a street in a Middle Eastern town when a Land Rover full of men pulled up next to me and the men jumped out and through car tyres over me from my feet to my head they then proceeded to pour petrol over me and set me on fire, another unpleasant death.

I think the most memorable was during the Second World War and my feeling is towards the end of the war. Firstly I am a member of a Lancaster Bomber crew in the operations room with the rest of the crew, Winston Churchill, Dwight D Eisenhower and Charles De-Gaul and we are being briefed for a special operation. My next vision the crew are walking toward a Lancaster Bomber and climbing on board in full flying gear. I take my place in the nose of the plane as front gunner. My next recollection is of the plane flying over I presume Germany it is very dark and cramped when the sky is lit up with flames and flashing lights, lots of smoke and then I hear a very big bang and everything went black. My next feeling is of my granddaughter Mini shaking me and telling me to wake up because I am having a dream.

Five of my dreams/ visions have been from 1944 to date and so if they were recollections of past lives then we must be multi- conscious beings, because there is no way I could have died five times in seventy years. I leave you to ponder on this, all I ask of you is to try and keep an open mind I do not pretend to fully understand. Can I add at this point the person I am named after died in a Lancaster Bomber just prior to the end of World War Two and I have always had a strong feeling even love for the Lancaster Bomber, as I say I will leave it up to you, dream or reality.

I find messages and inspirational writings come to me at all times of the day and night, sometimes they are short but occasionally they may be quite long. This was the case a few weeks ago; it was not the length of the writing which surprised me but from whom the message was from. Since her passing my wife Pat has visited me many times but to date she had never passed a message through me, so I was quite taken aback by this. However I would like to share it with you.

A Message from Pat.

That morning as I lay in my bed, I started to feel strange motion inside of me and beautiful Gold and White light began to surround me. I t was really lovely but I was fearful not really fully understanding what was happening to me. At this moment I realised that this was the time and that the dying process had begun.

I have various recollections of that day. I was visited by Alec and my friend Yvonne it was really nice to see her, the kids came and brought their dad with them bless them and I recall my sisters and my niece with their husbands. On the evening my earthly time was drawing to a close when a voice told me to calm down, everything was going to be all right, that he loved me, that all my family were with me, but one was missing and oh there she is driving up the motorway" be careful I told her, take your time". I opened my eyes and saw Alec, my lovely Alec holding my hand, comforting me, loving me and telling me it was time to go and then it was over and my soul was free of my earthly life.

My family got up and moved into the room next door and Alec went outside and stood composing himself before returning to sit with me. He sat on the other side of the bed and I held his hand" don't go just yet" I said I'm not quite ready", and we stayed for several minutes, I think he was surprise that I had held his hand. He then joined the rest of the family in the next room, everyone was very subdued talking of what had just happened. I followed Alec home and heard him saying to me" just give me a sign show me that you're alright, I will be ok if I know you are".

Well I went off to see the one person I knew he would believe, his sister in the North East of England. I stood before her looking radiant, as I did her phone rang and I left. Well I passed among them frequently even on the day of the funeral I was so proud of them all as they sat in church. My son's wife Tasha and my friend Joely read out beautiful words about me, I smiled as they talked and Alec putting his arms around each of them giving them the strength, they were so brave.

Well enough of that what I really want to say is this is brilliant I go visiting all of the family regularly passing among them, though most of the time they don't notice me. Alec has been a great help to me and I hope that I have helped him to come to terms with all of this. I won't embarrass him, he knows how much I love him.

I am pleased that all the kids have begun to get on with their lives as they must do. The grand children are brilliant and though I might not have been physically there I have not missed one single thing and if they read this they will know that I will always be around them.

Once I had crossed over one of my biggest surprises was my dad waiting for me with a boy, and I was introduced to my son, I had lost years before, his name is Philip and I loved the day when I took him to meet Alec his dad, it was very emotional as was my first meeting with Alec since my passing, we laughed, cried cuddled it was amazing.

Alec had always said that there was life after death but I didn't believe him. He once said if he went first he would find a way to come back and show me. Well it didn't quite work out the way he thought it would. Ha ha ha.

Seriously though I need to thank Yvonne's husband Paul for helping Alec to find his true self and to open the door for him, I know he won't turn back. To you dear Alec I know the tears you have shed writing this for me, but remember I will Love you forever.

Pat.

Now from the content of this message it was not meant for me but for the children and grandchildren a confirmation that she is always around them. That she has not missed out on any of the events after her passing and that she will always be there for them. Let me say I shed a lot of tears taking this message, however I was really pleased to do it for it confirmed to the family just how close she is to all of us.

Recently Pat's mum Dot passed away, she had been in a home since just before Pat passed and in the last year or so had not been in the best of health. She was a lovely lady yes she could be a bit feisty and I suppose that is where her daughter got it from, however I found her to be a very caring person. I didn't visit her too many times and when I did I would go with one of her remaining daughters, however I always took her chocolates, which we shared with the other residents, toward the end she wasn't fully aware of us but I would sit and talk to her for although her body was weak her soul was strong and that she would be able to hear me. I would also rub a chocolate across her lips so that although she couldn't eat them she would at least be able to taste them, she loved chocolate.

The day she passed I asked the universe if I would be allowed to see that she had arrived in heaven and that she had been met by family members. Well that evening as I was in my bed I saw a vision of Dot, Pat and Philip, the boy was jumping up and down I felt because his Nan had come to stay. As I have said before the spirit world is only next door and not a million miles away.

Well the fourth anniversary of Pat's passing came around and her daughter put a photograph of her and Pat on FB, with a caption saying something along the lines of I am not afraid of dying but I am frightened about what happens next, this took me aback really because we had talked about such things in the past, ok not in great depth but I thought she had understood me. The other thing that surprised me was that a lot of her friends felt the same way, I did suggest to her we might have a coffee night at mine with some of them and talk it through she declined saying it was very personal and didn't feel her friends would want to do it. Ok I decided to talk with Mary Magdalene and we decided to do a live broadcast on The Afterlife this way we would broach the subject with lots of people nearly 2 million as it turned out and a great success just under nine thousand hits on you tube in one day, amazing. I have not gone into detail re the programme however I have left details on how to listen at the end of the book, you should easily be able to find it if you wish to. On the anniversary of Pat's passing I wrote a small piece and I would like to share this with you. I wrote this for me but truly it's for everyone who has gone through this traumatic time. Love and Light Alec. xxx

In memory of my life's Love. RIP Pat. 3rd May 2011

Close your eyes my love, go to sleep for your earthly pain and existence draws to a close. Allow my love for you carry you forward toward eternal peace. Think not of our parting but of our universal existence, holding us together for all eternity. It matters not that I am here and you are there resting eternally. This love that bonds us together is the glue, the cement of the universe, energy so strong that nothing can ever separate us. So close your eyes my love, go to sleep.

So you see even after four years the feelings and the sense of loss are still very strong.

Chapter 6

WITH A LITTLE HELP FROM MY FRIENDS

This next chapter in this story started about fifteen months ago. As was usual I went to my Wednesday meeting and toward the end Paul told me he needed to talk with me and so he began to say that the spirit world was conspiring to bring my daughter and myself together again. Well my friends I was flabbergasted as he had no knowledge about me having a daughter. He went on to say that a younger and older spirit were organising a meeting between the two of us, I said to Paul after twenty five years with very little contact I couldn't see it happening. His reply was that it was time. I asked what do I have to do, he replied absolutely nothing it would all sort out with little help from me. Let me say in the many things Paul had told me he had never been wrong, so I sat back and waited.

Well it was at the end of November last year when I had a telephone call from her, she was quite upset in her mind about a lot of things but her main thought was that her mum who had passed many years before wanted her to join her on the other side. After listening to her for quite a while I began to explain to her that her mum would not under any circumstance want her to do anything that would bring about that situation and in fact it just wasn't the way spirit worked that they stay around us to help and encourage, not try and persuade us to join them. Our conversation lasted for quite a while but by the end of it things were much calmer.

A few nights later I was talking to Mary Magdalene on Skype and she felt that I was not right and worried about something , I explained that my daughter had been in touch and that she was disturbed over the happenings of the past. At that moment she told me that Jean her mum had come through and quite honestly she told me I had been an ass hole, (something to be honest I couldn't deny). However she went on to say that she had listened to my conversation with our daughter and was pleased with the way I had tried to help her. She also told me that she forgave me for the past and we both agreed that we had loved each other but our downfall had been a lack of understanding of each other's needs. She also went on to say that I certainly wasn't the same person as I had been all those years ago. My friends I received great healing that night and a lot of ghosts from the past were laid to rest.

On the 23rd of December 2014 Mary Magdalene and I broadcast a live radio show on the subject of Grief to be followed with a personal reading for my great friend Bob Williams. The show started as usual with a bit of banter between Mary Magdalene, Bob and me and then we went into the first part of the show with me reading out some words I had written earlier regarding grief. I then found myself talking about my own experience, let me say this was not the intention but the whole thing just seemed to follow on as I explained what I perceived to be the main stages of grief as I had experienced them. My friends I truly thought I had survived the grief of Pat's passing but my God by the end of this I knew I hadn't and the raw emotion and baring of the soul came over loud and clear, it certainly made fantastic listening and the later public response was immense.

After the interval Mary Magdalene went on to do the reading for Bob and again it proved to be a fantastic piece of radio. I know Bob won't mind me saying that he went into the reading with some doubts, but within a very short time his beautiful wife Maggie had come through and let him know in no uncertain terms that she wasn't happy with the way he washed or more to the point didn't wash or put away the dishes often enough, Bob's reply was that he had washed up before leaving the house, she replied with yes you washed them but you didn't dry them or put them away. Well if ever there was a defining moment when you know you are talking with spirit this was it for Bob new she was right and any disbelief was dispelled in that moment. She told him to stop being angry, that she had not left him, though she didn't have her physical body spiritually she was always with him and went everywhere with him. The reading continued with his wife telling him she had been with him on a cruise Bob and I had been on recently and she had watched him walking by the canals in Venice and had actually pushed a man into him to catch his attention but he was too moody to notice, again Bob knew this to be true, it was the day of his big birthday. I won't embarrass him by saying which but he couldn't get his wife out of his mind and it was upsetting him (it was at this moment I decided to ask Mary Magdalene to help him for although I do have the gifts I believe I am too close to my friend to help him).

Well after riding around the canals sightseeing we stopped by a cathedral as the gondola pulled into the side, Bob jumped off and walked very quickly into it, I followed him and found him sat on a pew crying, he asked if I could see her I told him I wished I could, but I couldn't lie yet at that moment in front of us appeared the most enormous red heart and I knew then that she was there, I told him but I don't think he heard so over-powering was his grief at that time. In the reading Maggie told him that she was stood at the entrance to the cathedral but we had both rushed past her. The reading finished Bob was calmer and a lot happier though it took a few weeks for it all to sink in with him but he has become a much calmer and happier person thanks to his message from the other side. That show went out to 1.8 million listeners and had 5500 hits in one day on you tube and hopefully many people had some healing that night. We also had emails from two people who told us that they wouldn't be here today if they had not listened to that programme for they were intent on harming themselves so I can only say how pleased we are that a lot of good things came from that programme, on a personal note it taught me to take one day at a time and to stop beating myself up with the grief, something perhaps others who are suffering should think about. One night whilst talking to my daughter I asked if she would like to talk with Mary Magdalene to see if it would help her, she agreed and so I set up a Skype meeting for her. The reading lasted for quite a long time but eventually she rang me and told me she would talk with me the next day. When we talked I had first to reassure her that I had not discussed her regarding anything with Mary Magdalene. She went on to say that her mum had been part of the reading and quite a lot of things were sorted out regarding me.

My daughter and I are now on a much sounder footing in our relationship and I can honestly say that I have now in my life someone whom I had given up hope of ever seeing again and I hope and pray this will go on forever and all thanks to two very good mediums and two very loving spirits.

On the fourth anniversary of Pat's passing Sue my step daughter posted photograph of her and Pat on Face Book, in the comments she wrote that she wasn't afraid of dying more about what comes next and quite a few of her friends responded in the same way. So I rang and asked Sue if it would help if I held a coffee night with some of her friends to discuss the subject, she declined on the basis it would be too much of a problem getting them all together. Well I talked with Mary Magdalene and we decided to do a show on the afterlife. This would take in various aspects of spirituality and so a live show was done that week. It is a fact that discussion within families, the church etc. is not to the front in topic of conversation and I believe in England we over protect our children to the extent many do not go to the funerals of family members who have passed over. So an open discussion that we did surprised me with the response, we had nearly 8000 hits on You Tube and absolutely loads of e-mails, both Mary Magdalene and I hope by doing these kinds of programmes it will help listeners realise there is far more to them than they readily perceive, it may take time and patience but we have an abundance of both.

Another programme followed with a theme of Letting Go. Whenever a traumatic event occurs in your life, no matter what it is whether its bereavement, divorce, or a romance/relationship coming to an end there are always people left behind. In the case of bereavement a husband, wife, son, daughter or other family members all of whom have to find a way to move on. This does not mean forgetting your loved one who has passed, but finding a place for them in your consciousness to allow you all to go forward, which you all must do. So if you can all let go of the emotion attached to the event that happened not the person who passed, and then you will all be able to move on, for it is the emotion that is holding you all there.

The same applies in relationships one or the other's feelings change the love stops and they move on, possibly straight into another relationship, but that is not necessarily so. The point is the other person invariably did not want this to happen and find themselves alone feeling unwanted and insecure, in truth a form of grief not dissimilar to someone passing. However the same thing applies they have to let go of the emotion so they too can move on along their pathway. I am not saying any of this is easy but to carry on and find new happiness it has to be done. Do not take all of this so called baggage with you it can only make your progression harder.

This programme was very successful and shows Mary Magdalene and I to be on the right road in wanting to help our fellow beings find their way through the hard time that can befall all of us.

It was during this time my friends that I once again received a large of personal healing from the Universe. I went to my bedroom and as I walked in to my astonishment I was met by a room full of golden orbs of light. I lay on the bed and one after the other came to me and showered me with streamers of golden light. When they had finished the room was left in darkness and I fell asleep. Next day I woke up to feelings of calm and inner peace and in truth a feeling of having received so much love and healing. Okay a vision dream whatever you make your own minds up of what happened, but I was not asleep when I walked into that bedroom filled with golden light. We cannot under estimate the power of the Universe the Heart and of course Love.

Chapter 7

SPIRITUAL HEALING

John.

Well my friends in the spring of this year I was invited along with my granddaughter Mini to visit some friends John and Anja who live in Rojales which is part of the district of Alicante in Spain. I have known John for some thirty years and we both worked in Financial Services for many years and it was through this connection that we met.

Through most of our time there John was not well and so Anja took it on herself to show Mini and I around the area. Because it was Easter week there were lots of parades going around the streets, Mini loved it as all the children were given sweets by the children in the parade. It was a very colourful and exciting time and the town had obviously put a lot of effort into the whole occasion.

A few days before we were due to travel back home john was telling me about his early life back in his home town of Huddersfield in Yorkshire. He went on to tell me his childhood had not been great because his dad had took a lot of interest in his younger brother and very little interest in him, telling him he was hopeless and would never do any good in his life and of course never gave him the love children would look for from their dad. At the same time he was telling his younger son how wonderful he was and how he would go on to achieve great things whilst lavishing his love on him. Well John has gone through his life feeling unloved and unworthy and of course through the feelings of being insecure his personal life had truly suffered not being able to show his love in the relationships that he had. Contrary to this his business life has been very successful. I was somewhat stunned when he told me these things as over the years I had always found John to be confident and a very amiable man. It just goes to show how we can hide our true feelings for long periods of time.

On the evening he showed me a black and white photograph of his dad and a group of men stood by an old van (probably wasn't that old in 1950's), John went on to tell me he was desperate to know what his dad (who had passed away some time previously) thought of the life he had made for himself and he asked if I would try and contact his dad for him. I agreed to try and help him.

Well that night I asked the universe if I could meet with Billy Stalker, John's dad as John was in need of some confirmations. As I sat there I began to hear Glen Miller music (In the mood) coming closer and closer, then an elderly man stood in front of me, he spoke just one word a name Ethel and then he disappeared immediately a black and white (spirit) cat jumped up on to my lap, and that you might say was that short and to the point.

The next day we went to lunch and as we sat around the table I discussed with John the happenings of the night before. I told John I had something but wasn't sure exactly what. I began by telling him about the Glen Miller music, John was very surprised and told me his dad had been a big band leader who travelled all over the country and that he loved Glen Miller's music and would sometimes play it to the audiences. I mentioned the ladies name and she was his dad's mum john's grandmother. When I mentioned the black and white cat John nearly fell off his chair as he explained his dad loved the cat and never went anywhere without taking the cat including all his travels with the band. All I could say was well it's certainly with him now.

John was a bit subdued and asked if his dad had said anything to say about him. I told him no but the very fact he had turned up and gave me some confirmation of who he was that John recognised showed that he did care and although he didn't say much about his son's successes he did come. I believe a certain amount of healing came from the message, but nothing in comparison to the healing John would get in the October of this year.

Although John spends a lot of time in Spain and also with his friend Anja in Sweden and Finland he has cause to also spend time in England and this year I was able to return his hospitality by having come and stay with me.

As usual on a Tuesday evening UK time Mary Magdalene and I set about recording Friday night's programme. I was telling her I had John staying and so the two of them chatted for a while then John went to sit in the lounge leaving us to get on with the recording. The show we had decided was to be on Spiritual healing and how and what the benefits can be for people suffering from the loss of someone close to them. We had barely go started when Mary Magdalene told me John's dad Billy had come through to her and had a message for John so we took a quick break and I went to get John. Having got back into the office we started again and she delivered the message to John. This is not the exact wording but his dad told him that he was sorry his intention had never been to do him down as he had known from John's birth that his son was very special and strong of will and mind. Whereas his other son was the opposite and so he had built up the other boy's confidence by doing John down. He realised now what a terrible disservice he had done John and could see how his treatment had prevented John from having loving, caring relationships. He agreed he was wrong, he thought John was much the stronger of the two boys and did not understand the damage it would do to him.

I must say John was quite stunned and shocked at what his dad told him but by the end of the message John had received a terrific amount of spiritual healing. It may take months for all of it to sink in but knowing John he will take great comfort, knowing that his dad did love him and that he was sorry for the way he had treated him. My take on this is that his dad in spirit would receive as much healing as John. In a recent conversation with John he told me that he had not listened to the tape recording of the radio programme until he had been back home in Spain for several days and now was able to feel some of the healing he had received from his dad's message.

Love and Light.

A sure sign of John's spiritual awakening was this poem which I would like to share with you.

Evocative

I may never see tomorrow, there's no written guarantee
And things that happened yesterday, belong in history
I cannot predict the future, I cannot change the past
I have just the present moment, I must treat it as my last
I must use this moment wisely, for it will soon pass away
And it will be lost to me forever, as part of yesterday
I must exercise compassion, help the fallen to their feet
Be a friend to the friendless, make an empty life complete
The unkind things I do today, may never be undone
Any friendship that I fail to win, may never more be won
I may not have another chance, on bended knee I pray
And I thank God with humble heart, for giving me the day.

Anonymous

Cathy & Margaret

At the beginning of 2015 a friend called Cathy came home from visiting her family in Australia. I met her the day after and she was absolutely distraught as she explained her dad had passed over in the night and she desperately needed to know that he was alright. I assured her that I would try and contact him. Well my friends that night I asked the universe if I could speak with him so that I could reassure his daughter of his wellbeing.

As I drifted off to sleep I found myself watching a vision of a young man in a Fun Palace/Café type of establishment with lots of the old 1950's type one armed bandit machines and he was saying to a young girl "stick with me and you will be alright". Next thing I am being shown racing cars going round a circuit again the cars seemed to represent the 1950's. A man's face appeared much older than the previous younger man and he looked at me and said "tell ma gal I'm alright" and he then disappeared only to reappear with another man wearing a white polo neck sweater and sporting a very neatly trimmed beard. His hair was black as was his beard. The other man seemed to be slightly behind this chap and I realised that they were showing me who had met Cathy's dad when he passed over.

A few days later I met Cathy and told her of my vision and what her dad had said. She seemed relieved to know that he was alright but couldn't understand the visions as her mum Margaret had met her dad later on in their lives. With a funeral pending in Australia Cathy was flying back there and said she would ask her mum. She took a copy of my first book Granddad you have a Message with her to give to her mum and I hoped it would give her some peace and reassurance about the afterlife, even though I doubted that it would stop her missing the physical him.

After another visit to Australia I met up with Cathy again and she told me that her mum had had contact with her dad's sister and she confirmed the information that her dad had given and so the visions were confirmation from her dad for his family to know that he had come through for them.

Since then Cathy's mum has visited Sutton Coldfield and I know she won't mind me saying that although she still has a long way to go in the grieving process she at least knows that her beloved husband is safe and well in the land of spirit, and so the healing goes on. It was with great pleasure that I was able to welcome both Cathy and Margaret to the launch of my latest book "Through the eyes of a Child" at the end of September this year. Another story of where the world of spirit helps another family to come to terms with their physical loss.

Love and Light.

Denise & family

In February of 2015 my nine year old granddaughter Mini and I travelled to Nailsea in Somerset to spend a week with my son Dave, his wife Tasha and my grandson Ethan. We had only been there an hour when we had a phone call to say that Josh the son of Dave's stepsister Denise had been killed in a road accident near Lichfield in Staffordshire. To say that everyone was shocked would be an under- statement. I was asked by Michelle, Mini's mum not to tell Mini about Josh and as Mini was using her mum's phone to be aware that there may be some sympathy txt messages. Because Dave could not accommodate both Mini and me and so Tasha's mum Eve had agreed to me staying with her in Weston – Super- Mare.

Although I only met Josh once at a family gathering, that night I asked the universe if I could see him so that I could confirm that he had arrived safely into the world of spirit and then I would talk to his mum and the rest of the family to give them some peace of mind at this very difficult time. Well I went to my bed hoping Josh would come to me and I was not disappointed, within a very short time he stood smiling in front of me and with him stood a young lady dressed in a black trouser suit and who had the most amazing hair style. No words were spoken just the smile and then the vision faded away. In truth I was very happy that on the very day he had passed he had come through, he so wanted his mum and family to know that he was all right. The puzzling thing for me was, who was the young woman I was aware that Josh was Denise's oldest child but felt the young woman was also one of josh's siblings (I needed to find out) she must have been very close to him to have met him when he passed over. The next night Josh came again this time on his own and confirmed to me he was all right. I couldn't see any injuries on him though I felt pain in my head and down the left side of my body, which I thought was from the accident. Once again the vision faded and I fell asleep. A few days later Mini started to receive txt messages on her mum's phone, so it was decided that we would tell her the news of Josh's passing, she took the news very well and although she is a very sensitive caring girl and took the news very well she did not cry. I told her it was ok to cry if she wanted to but she said " I am ok ", I gave her a hug and told her if she wanted to talk about it I was there for her and she carried on playing as before.

When we arrived home later that week I rang Michelle and asked if

Denise had possibly lost a baby two or three years before Josh was born, the thought that the young woman was a sibling felt very strong in my mind and I needed to know. She couldn't tell me but agreed to try and find out. A few hours later she rang me and confirmed Denise had indeed miscarried two years previous to Josh being born. Now I could talk with Denise.

A few days later I met Jane, Denise's sister and we had a conversation about the things that had happened she gave me Denise's phone no. and a few hours later I rang her. She was surprised with my message but I felt some relief in her voice, not just with the message but by talking with someone who knew what she was going through we made friends on FB and I began to support her and the family whenever I could, I don't think Denise will mind me saying that at this time she was very angry and full of guilt as to what had happened to Josh and I talked her through the emotions we all have when someone we love passes to the world of spirit. We all ask why but if we can try and understand it is not the end of life, but a moving on into the next stage of our eternal existence the human experience being a temporary stop over (so to speak) on the journey.

On Josh's next appearance to me he showed me a vision of a multi-coloured collage hanging on the wall in his mum's living room and told me this is what he wanted to give his family good memories of him and a reminder to them that he was always around them. I rang Denise and told her what Josh wanted. The collage through her for a moment until she remembered his favourite T shirt which was lots of vivid colours and of course it now hangs in a frame on the living room wall just as he wanted. He also told me to tell her not to feel angry as it was preventing him from reaching her.

I decided to ask Mary Magdalene if she would have a talk with Denise and she agreed so I set up a meeting on Skype for her at my home. On the day Denise arrived with my daughter Michelle and after introducing them to Mary Magdalene the meeting began. As I was not party to the readings I will relate to you what they told me.

Firstly Josh told his mum to stop being so angry, that he was with her all the time, but he found the house strange because there was no fun anymore. He told her to watch out for her daughter Billie because she was really struggling to come to terms with his death and if she didn't look to her Billie would cause all sorts of problems in the future, Denise told me Josh was thrilled that the picture had been placed on the wall, but his main message was one of love. Our Michelle told me her mum Pat had come through for her and had told her she was an amazing mother to her children, Michelle asked Josh if she would someone who would make her happy, he laughed and told her he loved her because of the way she was and said of course she would if she got rid of the smell of horses (we think he meant take a shower and use perfume). I firmly believe this was the start of a lot of healing for both girls, Mary Magdalene told me later that Josh had had her in tears as he insisted on singing a song to her. As always these readings take time for the heart and mind to sort out, but at least they had got what they both came for. I continued to keep in touch with Denise offering help and understanding. Another meeting was arranged with Mary Magdalene for Denise and Billie and once again I left them to talk with her.

Afterwards Denise, Billie and I discussed the reading Josh had told Billie how much he missed their fooling around together, that he loved her very much, that he would like to see the house go back to how it used to be, full of fun. He told his mum that she needed to stop blaming and having nasty thoughts about the van driver, that it was an accident and in fact the whole thing had been agreed in the contract prior to him being born. He also told her a family holiday would be good as he could go with them. He also thought moving house would be a possibility for them as it might help them all get through the grieving. His words for his dad were he loved him and new he would get through this in his own way.

In my mind this is a family that has great love for each other and again the benefits of this reading will take several weeks if not months for them to fully digest. The time has moved on since the reading but I recently spent some time with the family and I believe the healing process is underway slowly but you know this is a marathon not a sprint. I am however convinced this very brave family will eventually come through this with great dignity and of course due to their courage and a lot of spiritual healing from their son.

Neil.

Well I have known Neil since he was a thirteen year old boy, at the time I got involved with the organisation of the town's carnival and Neil was a willing helper. In the time I have known him he has always been a big person in size if not in stature. Some years ago we lost touch with each other and it was not until before Pat's passing that we connected again.

During his working life Neil had been a self- employed car valet of some standing and also cleaned large industrial trucks at an open cast coal mine. It was during this time that he was struck down with cancer of the throat and thyroid gland. He went into hospital expecting to be back at work within six months but actually he has not been able to return to his job. For whatever the reasons he suffers from severe back pain and due to this and other things, medicinal drugs etc. his weight has gone from over weight to excessively over weight. During this time I have taken him to various hospitals, who have tried to solve his problems without much success. At the last visit I realised that to my mind they were merely paying Neil lip service and I just could not allow this to happen, so I asked if they minded me saying a few words, they agreed and I told them that in all the time we had been going there I could not see any improvement in Neil's health, in fact the opposite was the case where he was now worse than when he first started going. They did not disagree with me. On our way home from that meeting I told Neil in no uncertain terms that if he ever wanted to get back to normality in his life, he needed to take his life into his own hands and not depend on other people. This might sound harsh but I truly believe God helps them that helps themselves, Neil is like a son to me and I knew unless he started to sort himself out he was probably going to die.

After this incident Neil rang the hospital and told them in no uncertain terms he wanted his case seen at another hospital. This was done and Neil saw a doctor who had a totally different attitude to Neil. He told him exactly what he thought about Neil's health and what he expected Neil to do about it., which was to stop smoking, get regular exercise and to lose weight and gave him three months to get on with it. He weighed Neil and told him he expected him to lose two stone in three months and so Neil had some choices to make.

I decided to arrange a Skype meeting for Neil with Mary Magdalene and myself and what came out of this reading was how low Neil's self-esteem was, that he felt since his childhood he had not been loved and although he threw love into his family home life it was not reciprocated. This has had a damaging effect on him and his relationships with other people and of course his weight got heavier as he spent years comfort eating. During the reading he was told by Mary Magdalene what a beautiful soul and loving person he is. The main theme was to stop throwing love at the people who didn't seem to be able to put the same love his way. This did not mean that he should shun them or not see them, but just to not go over the top with his love.

Since then Neil has joined a gym reduced his smoking and eating comfort food and began to regain his confidence. He is a much happier person and although he may have a long way to go he is at least on the right road now. At last he has made decision for himself and is beginning to reap the benefits. The story here is about a man's battle with his mind and the belief that he was unworthy, the truth, he is a beautiful soul who will give help wherever it is needed and is hopefully now on a road to recovery.

I would like to thank Neil for allowing his story to be told in the hope that it might help someone else in a similar predicament.

John and Julie.

Well my friends it always seems to happen how the Universe has a way of putting people in front of you for a purpose and so it was at the beginning of last year. It began with my Wi- fi router playing up, so I rang my supplier and had a chat with a service engineer I explained the problem he checked my telephone line told me no problem with that so he would send an engineer the next day to my house. The next morning the said engineer came to the house, he was a tall, stocky man who had a quietness about him. Almost immediately I sensed the need to talk with him I was being told by the universe that he needed help. Well he checked the outside telephone line and then went into my office to check the Wi-Fi router, again I'm being told to give him one of my books (a copy of my first Granddad book) he took it off me as I explained to him about some of my "gifts". As we were talking I noticed the spirit of a young lady stood directly behind him and I asked "if a young woman in spirit probably in her early twenties means anything to you as she isn't connected to me". He started to cry and explained that due to circumstances at the time he and his wife had terminated a pregnancy and neither of them had been able to get over the guilty feelings of their action, that they never discussed it for fear of upsetting each other and on the anniversary of the event they didn't even talk to each other and this had gone on for years.

"Well" I said "your daughter is saying to you that she loves you both but enough is enough the guilt has gone on too long and it is time to stop and forgive yourselves, stop beating yourselves up I am ok it is time for you both to move on."

Having completed the job it was time for him to go he thanked me for my help, I asked if he was alright as I think he was still in shock as he walked back to his van. My friends, this is not easy and the responsibility is immense, but a message must be passed on and this family desperately needed to hear this one. That evening I had a personal message on FB from a lady who actually turned out to be Julie, John's wife and she said "Hello you don't know me but thank you for accepting me onto your FB page my husband came to you today the BT engineer. Thank you for the book I am sitting here in tears typing this but so thankful for what you told him as I have spent 25 years with regret for what happened and I have never forgave myself with the passing of my mom 18months ago my life has been in limbo much love and thank you again I'm reading your book now " I replied "Hi Julie, thank you sometimes the universe throw people at us for various reasons at unexpected times, which is how it was today the moment he walked through the door I knew it wasn't just the phone that needed fixing. Below is a page from the next Granddad book I hope it helps you as much as it has helped me over the last 3 months, bringing my long lost daughter back into my life after 30 years of waiting.

God Bless. Alec.

Forgiveness.

Love and Forgiveness go well together in as much as you cannot love anyone if you don't love yourself. Forgiveness mirrors this, you cannot forgive anyone if you cannot forgive yourself.

Neither of these emotions is easy, but remember, every being comes to earth to learn and this means making mistakes. Therefore it follows that in the making of mistakes other beings may get hurt, this includes you. So it follows to forgive yourselves for the mistakes or wrong doing you do, will help you understand others and allow you to forgive them. Have no doubt of this; forgiveness is one of the main attributes for you to ascend to Eternal life.

For this is the way.

Well Julie went on to say "Thank you Alec. To know she is happy has taken such a weight off me it is untrue." Well my friends once again we are being told to let go of the grief, the pain, the hurt and the guilt of the past, these are the lessons we came here to learn and experience, and now we must carry on with our life's journey as was intended.

Love and Light.

Lynne- Marie.

Ever since the night a few months after Pat passed away and I sat in Lynne's house discussing a new mortgage with her and her husband Sean, Lynne asked how I was coping. I started to tell her about all the strange and wonderful things that were happening to me. I sensed Sean was thinking I had lost my mind and so I asked him if that was the case. He told me actually no he didn't as he too had experienced many strange things whilst growing up and as an adult but until this day he had not mentioned it to anyone not even Lynne. The truth of it is Sean has an ability or gift to see into the future and uses the gift from time to time, he told us when Lyn miscarried several years earlier she might have died but he knew she was going to be alright because he could see them together many years in the future. After this night

Lynne would periodically ask if I could "see" anything or anyone around her, well I couldn't say yes if I didn't see anything and this has gone on for some time now so it was obvious she was still grieving over the loss of her child.

Well a few months ago while travelling back from North Wales for some reason which I cannot explain the thought came in my mind that I should ask the universe to help me contact Lynne's child in spirit as I felt she needed to know if her daughter in was ok, her name is Keira. That night a young girl in spirit came to see me she was about ten years old and as I have known Lyn since she was born I knew this girl was her daughter as she was the image of her mum at that age. She told me to tell her mum that she was well and that she loved her. I have to say at this point I also felt a male energy which I thought was Lynne's son. So the next day I rang Lynne and asked to meet up with her and so I went for coffee at her home. I started by telling her that I had seen and spoke with Keira, that she was ok and had sent her love, that she was around her family all the time and thought one of her Lynne's son's may have seen her. I also mentioned my feelings of a male energy, this surprised Lynne and she told me that when she miscarried Keira she had also lost a son and so my feelings were proved to be correct and also confirmed to Lynne that Keira had come through for her.

A few nights later both Keira and the boy came to see me expressing concern that their mum was drinking too much in her need to come to terms with their passing and feared she might do herself harm. They insisted I talk to her. Well not the easiest of messages to pass on, I have known Lynne a long time and never felt there was a problem. Well I talked with Lynne, she listened to me but felt their concerns were unfounded and I must say I tend to agree with her however the spirit world does not lie so I suppose if they love her any habit would be of concern. The theme to this story is the relief and peace of mind that Lynne has knowing her children in spirit are alright, but also that the spirit world does have love and concerns about us that are left behind to continue on our journey.

Love and Light.

Marilyn.

A friend called me and asked if I would talk with a client of hers who had lost her daughter and was having difficulty in coming to terms with it. I told my friend I was not a qualified bereavement counsellor and was not sure that I could help her. My friend replied you are a man who has gone through this very thing and understands so you are more than qualified, so I told her to ask the lady to ring me and I would talk with her.

Marilyn did ring me and we arranged that she would come to my home. When she arrived I looked into her eyes they appeared to be void of any life no sparkle just desolation. I showed her into the lounge, got us a drink and I began to explain my situation about not being a qualified counsellor when in my mind I could hear Pat saying" for God's sake shut up and let the woman talk" so I told Marilyn what had just happened and I asked her to talk to me.

She told me that her daughter Katrina had been running the London half marathon eight years earlier when she collapsed and died, Marilyn could not come to terms with the thought that she should have been there with her daughter which considering her age would I think have been an impossibility. However she was consumed with guilt and found herself in an emotional bubble she didn't seem to be able to get out of this situation wasn't helped when a few years later her friend and neighbour Graham passed away. To make matters worse her other children and grandchildren and son in law were all caught in the same bubble afraid to move on in case they hurt her feelings. This told me Marilyn was in a very delicate state not helped by the fact she suffers also with Bi-Polo and I asked her if she had sought professional help, she said she had talked with a bereavement counsellor but had not seemed to gain anything from it. I suggested talking things through might help to release some of the anger and grief she was suffering and suggested if she wanted to come and talk I was prepared to listen. She told me she would like to do that and so it was arranged we would meet at my home every two weeks.

We started by talking about her daughter, what had she been like, her work etc. I told her that my view was that Katrina was always with her and was concerned by the way her mum felt. The guilt etc. about not being with her that day when in fact there was no way that she could have been with her. The meeting always took the form of a chat which became more intense as the weeks went by. Some days I would show her some of my writing and let her read it, usually stuff that was appropriate to what we had talked about on any given visit.

We would talk about her other children and grandchildren, how they were coping etc. She knew they were suffering because they couldn't get on with their lives in case they hurt her, but at this time she did not know how to help them. When Katrina's husband found someone else to love this was difficult although in her heart she knew it was right and of course now they all get on well together. As the weeks went by the changes though very slow began to take place. For me there was lots of stuff going on especially when in December I launched my first book.

Well the months rolled by and one day Marilyn said to me she felt that she had moved on just a little bit. I knew things were getting better for her but it is one thing for me to feel it but coming from her it was a fantastic moment I was so happy for her. After a few more chats she didn't come again and I felt pleased for her that she now felt she could cope. This story is not about the spirit world intervening it's about someone prepared to spend time listening and someone prepared to talk through the fears and guilt of her situation and accept that life is not always what it appears to be.

In August of this year Marilyn rang me and asked if I could visit her as she needed to talk with me, so we arranged the time and I called round to her house, my friends I was amazed at the transformation in her, her eyes were bright and alive her whole being was so different her positivity as she explained how her life had turned around, she was able to talk to her daughter Katrina and had found her faith again. I was so pleased for her and told her so she replied it would not have been possible but for me, I was humbled all I had done was listen she had done everything else herself.

The thing about this story is a whole family were caught in an emotional bubble unable to move in case they hurt their mum. Where by Marilyn in taking control of her emotions released everyone from that bubble. I am so proud of her courage in doing that and also in allowing me to write this story.

She has asked if the following words of love and inspiration written by her dad to her mum a long time ago can be part of her story, so please read on.

A personal letter from Charles Frederick Smith to his wife on their wedding anniversary. 1940:

My dear Mary,

Kindly accept this little gift in remembrance of our wedding day, looking back dear we have a lot to be thankful to Almighty God for. We have both had a good measure of health and strength, and are blessed with two lovely children and they too have their health and strength. I too must thank God for blessing my life with a good wife, thank you my dear for your kindness, perfect loyalty and true love to me. You have helped me more than I could express in paper and ink or words. You have helped me in a thousand ways to live a better and richer life, you have helped by words of love and deeds of kindness. Please accept my sincere thanks which come from the depths of my heart. My love for you dear still grows richer, I have not been able to give you worldly riches, but thank God dear we have had enough and a little to spare. We have each other to cheer us on life's way and no power on earth can take it away. I just felt that I must write this rather short letter of deepest thanks to my dear wife I assure you it is from the heart of your loving husband, who loves you dearly.

Fred. xxx.

I wonder how many wives have received such a beautiful letter of love and inspiration.

Love and Light. Alec.

Tom and Joely.

So my friends we come to the last of these short examples of spiritual healing and the one thing that binds all of these stories together and that is the love that was shared between the people concerned.

Well I have known Joely since she was a small child, however this story is about Joely the young woman who had an awful amount of responsibility thrust upon her. Firstly whilst in a relationship she became pregnant and gave birth to a beautiful baby girl she named Kelly. Her partner at the time decided this was not for him and he left them, the child was no ordinary baby and was diagnosed with a childhood cancer Neuro-Blastomer a killer disease if not treated properly. The family being a close knit unit looked to and after them and when it was put to Joely that her daughter might have to go to the USA for specialist treatment they all began various means of fundraising to begin putting the money together.

When Kelly was three years old Joely met and fell in love with Tom a young man full of energy, running his own business and he set about increasing various ways of raising the funds. Not long after meeting Joely, Tom himself was affected by what eventually was diagnosed as a brain tumour. Not to be deterred Tom and Joely with the help of other people and organisation carried on with a new found vigour to raise the funds for Kelly. During this time Kelly's cancer went into remission whilst Tom's tumour became more aggressive and eventually his prognosis became terminal. So here we have a young man given a virtual death sentence, pick up the pace with Joely to raise the money for Kelly's treatment before he died, the raising effort went viral in local and the national media and the £500,000 target to help Kelly began to become a reality.

Well in 2014 Tom and Joely got married and in 2015 the fund reached its target, however by this time Tom's health had deteriorated and he was close to passing over and their lives went into a very personal mode of caring for Tom, all of us who have been through this awful situation will know just how traumatic and painful it is.

The spiritual aspects of these events for me started in the most dramatic and amazing way, I was on holiday at the time and was going to my room when I started to experience strange feelings. To start I felt as though my head was leaving my body and then I thought I was going to pass out, I eventually fell onto my bed and closed my eyes, instantly I found myself in a room of light with Tom and Joely. My first thought was that Tom had passed away but what I couldn't understand was what Joely was doing there, Tom asked me various questions about his concerns of what happens when he passes and we talked about family members who might be there to meet him. I did however tell him that no matter what he was to follow the light and he would be shown the way and receive healing. He also talked to Joely about what he would like her to do once he passed over which was to look after herself and the children, to go on a bib holiday and to find love again as she was far too young to be on her own. His wife didn't want him to go and felt she might go with him, the love between them was immense. I explained to her that was not possible and of course she had the children to consider and look after. My friends at this point I woke up (so to speak) ,later a colleague told me this was not a meeting of spirit but a meeting of souls, hence Joely being there and my funny turn on the way to my room was my body preparing for my soul to join Tom and Joely. I text Joely's mum to find out how Tom was and she replied very very ill and that his time was near.

My friends throughout this book I have said about strange things happening and this experience was certainly one of the strangest.

On the evening of the day Tom passed away I was to record a radio programme with Mary Magdalene, she noticed I seemed a bit subdued and asked what was bothering me, I told her of Tom's passing, she asked if I wanted to go ahead with the recording I said yes and we made a start. Well virtually straight away she said a man was coming through to her and she felt that it was Tom with a message for Joely. He went on to say how much he loved her and how he had not wanted to leave her but that she should do all the things they had discussed, to do a family holiday and he would be with her, that she was to love again as she was to beautiful a person to spend the rest of her days on her own he then held out both hands and said that he would love her forever and asked us to make sure she got the message so that she knew he was ok on the other side.

Mary sent me a copy of the message and I forwarded it to Joely via her mum. A few nights later Tom came to me saying the message hadn't been delivered to Joely and it was imperative that she got it. I then sent another email to Joely's mum telling her to give her daughter the message, later that day she replied saying Joely had read the message but didn't believe it. The whole idea of Tom's message was to heal his wife's pain and make the coming weeks leading up to the funeral less painful, doing much the same as Pat showing herself to my sister on the day she passed away. You will recall I talked of this earlier in the book.

At the funeral I met up with Joely and although nothing was said about the message I knew she had not received it.

Recently Joely contacted me re some strange happenings that she was experiencing and I had a chance to talk to her about Tom and his message. I am pleased to say she now has the copy of the message and Tom's wish has been fulfilled. Better late than never I suppose.

Can I say at this point being able to receive messages from people who have passed over can be quite harrowing for the messenger if the receiving person does not believe, but I feel a responsibility to pass the messages on.

My friends the above have been just a few of the instances where the world of spirit and loved ones who have passed over come to our aid to help us come to terms with our lives and I probably more than most have plenty to be grateful for.

Chapter 8

FROM THE DARK INTO THE LIGHT

Well my friend when I set out on this journey the idea was to log all the strange and wonderful things that have happened since my much loved Pat passed over, and of course it has been a tremendous healing curve for me personally (and I truly hope for you too). However the thing that has surprised me most is the fact that not only has it done that but it has also been a journey of self- discovery, of finding my true self. My mum used to say to me "you are always looking for something" and of course I have now found what and who I was looking for!! ME!! , who I am, what I am have all come to light in the pages of this book. I am not just a human being, I am a cosmic being, I am an empath, a psychic, a medium and a healer. However the astonishing thing is the realisation that this is who I have been since the day I was born.

As a child at school and throughout my life I have shown empathy and understanding toward others to some people I may have appeared soft, but actually it was a sign of tremendous inner strength. I recall being caught in a really bad snow storm when I was about eleven years old and was so determined to get home safely, again this inner strength coming out of me. Throughout my life during times of stress caused by problems I had created for myself that inner strength would always see me through.

Again as a child living in a rural area I recall picking up various plants and seeing the black energy line around the shape of the leaves (using my imaginary third eye) or listening to music on the radio with my dad, I would start singing a song and sure enough that song would be the next one to be played "how do you do that" he would ask, but I couldn't tell him how I knew, I just knew.

That out of body experience when I was eleven years old, I did not understand why but I knew it had happened and no doubt it would happen again at some time in the future. From an early age I always saw faces / people in my sleep I just thought I was dreaming, of course I realise now that they were not dreams. What I am to put across to you is this has been a journey of re-discovery, a remembering of who and what I really am. I think during our lifetime we are taught so much nonsense, we wrap loads of guilt and other rubbish around our being that we forget who we are and what wonderful gifts we are blessed with and it sometimes takes a life changing experience for us to find our way to the inner truth, of who we are. I would add there are people who find their way without having to go through a trauma as I have, but have recognised their abilities all along. I feel that the following words from my first book are very appropriate at this point, so if you don't mind I would like to share them with you.

Journey through Life.

And as you journey through life all is well you feel that at last you've finally "cracked" it so to speak, when suddenly "Bang" that light at the end of the tunnel "wasn't" and you find your -self in the abyss, the darkness, the depths of despair. Now is the time your whole life as you knew it stops. Now is the time for you to look within and find your inner- being, use your intuition and you will see a flicker of light in the darkness use it to start and recreate the new journey, for surely this moment is one of those cross roads or even a dead end to what was and now you must move forward again one step at a time regaining the belief in your-self, to create a different but better life than what may have been. Not forgetting the past, but never the less carrying on, on your journey of life.

For this is the way.

Love and Light.

06/09/2013 at 03-05 hrs.

I think one of the most important things in the whole grief process is that your life must go on and you have to find the way of letting go, not of the person you have lost but letting go of all the pain, anxiety, anger and guilt that goes with your loss. Of course I believe that the Universe puts events, people and places in front of you and this in turn gives you choices that have to be made. It is important that you ask your inner being to help you chose the right direction to take for making a wrong choice will leave you on the wrong path.

It was during 2014 that Pat's sister Cilla was diagnosed with Leukaemia, at first things went well with her treatments and the prognosis was good however as we entered 2015 things began to deteriorate. At this time I decided to start going and staying with them in North Wales on a regular basis. Over the coming months I tried to help and support them in many ways a bit of cooking talking hopefully inspiring and generally helping out. We sometimes discussed her illness and thoughts on the afterlife fortunately both were believers in such things. We would also do small amounts of healing for as the months progressed tensions sometimes got a little heated which of course under the circumstances was quite normal. It was generally acknowledged that Bill was not a great cook or a great organiser but between Cilla and myself we got him to do cooking to a reasonable standard which in the fullness of time would prove to be very useful. By Christmas it was obvious Cilla's health was deteriorating and we spent more time together with me travelling more often than had been previously the case. On New Year's Day I channelled some writing which when I had finished I realised this message was for me and I have include it for you to read below.

Change in direction.

So my beautiful beings of Love and Light please understand that from time to time and particularly at this time of the year, the Universe will put different situations in front of you, it may be a place, a person or an event whichever this is a time of choices your choices. If you are undecided ask your inner self for a wrong choice can take you in a totally different direction to the one destiny intended. Believe that for you this is a time of change to what you have been and a correction to your life's journey, so go with what your heart and soul tells you to do, for in the majority of times change is for the better and the feeling in your soul is never wrong.

For this is the way.

The meaning of this message was that it was time for me to move on. I knew that the children had all found themselves and had moved on in their lives and were all happy with families of their own and I now realised that I wanted to try and rebuild certain parts of my life which to say the least I had found difficult in the past, my main problem being my home which to all intents and purpose was still very much Pat's home and probably always would be.

I have not been able to comfortably take another female there nor would I be able have another partner live with me there. Well on the second of January I started looking for a property in Holyhead. After a long discussion with Bill and Cilla I decided to go home and put my beautiful family home up for sale and then go and look for a property in Holyhead to live in.

It was during this time that Cilla was taken into hospital and she succumbed to the terrible illness and she passed quietly away to the land of spirit on the 27th February 2016 at 18:35. On the 11th February 2016 my son Dave, his wife Natasha and my daughter Michelle travelled to Bangor in North Wales for Cilla's funeral. There were many people in the church, a sign of how popular and loved she was. Well my friend's that brings me fairly well to today and so I would like to leave you with one more piece of writing about some of the inspirational people I have met along the way.

I always knew 2016 would be a year of much change and so it has proven to be. My property sale fell through and with that my house purchase in Holyhead did too. I suppose some things are just not meant to be. However I still continued to journey to North Wales and stayed with Bill helping and supporting him during the difficult time that he was going through, although at times many memories of Pat's passing was brought to the front of my mind.

(Me in Holyhead amongst the beautiful scenery)

During this period our earth's energy was being given a large surge of universal energy and a lift in the earth's vibration began as the two energies mixed together. This certainly effected my own vibration as I found out one evening in March. I walked into my bedroom to find the room was full of golden orbs not small like I was used to seeing but absolute enormous ones, I was amazed to say the least and to be honest my friend I had not seen the likes of these before. Well I climbed into my bed and the orbs began to move slowly toward me, as each one hovered above my head they showered me with sheds of golden light. This went on for quite some time with each orb coming to me until I eventually fell asleep. The next morning I awoke and felt that I had received an enormous amount of love and healing. I felt truly blessed.

A few days later I stood in front of a photograph of Pat and asked her to let me know if she was happy with my intention to leave the family home and move to North Wales. That evening I was going to see a medium friend Stephen Holbrook doing mediumship at the Castle Hotel in Tamworth, so I rang my daughter Michelle to see if she would like to join me, she did and so we arranged to meet at the venue, I told her the event started at 7-30pm and not to be late. Actually I don't know why I asked her to be there on time because she was never on time for anything but I felt it was important for her not to miss the start. As I finished the call I could hear Pat singing "I will always love you" and I understood that my earlier question to her had in fact been answered.

Well I arrived at the hotel stood talking to Stephen and his brother whilst keeping a watchful eye on the time, Stephen noticed this and asked was I waiting for someone, I told him my daughter who was usually late. He told me not to worry and set a table aside for us just to one side of the main audience. Well 7-30pm came and Stephen started to work, at this moment Michelle arrived with a friend and I was relieved because I felt it was important for her to be there. After his first reading he started talking about a young man who had passed 12 months before, well Michelle's hand went up straight away as she recognised this to be her cousin Josh who had passed exactly one year to the day in a road accident. After much banter between them

Stephen said that a female energy had come through and was saying her birthday was in September she also said her husband's birthday was in March which is my birthday so we now had Pat connecting with us. She told us that I was not the only spiritual person in the family, that our granddaughter was also gifted. My friend let me say I knew because my granddaughter and I had discussed about it some weeks before. Pat went on to say that 2016 would see big changes within the family and I realised that this was her confirmation of what I had asked earlier in the day. My friend I felt truly elated that I had had such a positive response to my question.

Well April 1st found me on the ferry from Holyhead to Dublin with some friends I had recently met in Tamworth at Mac's house, they were on holiday visiting friends and lived in the Bahamas. The reason for visiting Ireland was to go to a gathering of likeminded people who I met on Social Media, originally there was to be ten of us travelling however for one reason or another only the three of us made the trip and I must say Dave and Erica were great company, I also couldn't help but notice the likeness between Erica and Pat it was uncanny.

(Myself, Dave & Erica)

The event in Carlow was not as well attended as we thought it would be so after dinner it was decided to hold the event at the home of Kirsten and Dave who in fact had put a lot of time and effort into the organisation of the evening. I must say the night was a great success and the spiritual energy generated in the room was absolutely awesome some of us actually became very emotional. That night I met a lot of people I had only talked to on Facebook, perhaps it was my own naivety but I was surprised that I was recognised as an inspirational writer and author, something I had not given much credence to in the past. During the evening I was introduced to a lady whom I had had several discussions with on Facebook in the past, but had lost touch with and I must say I felt as though a meeting of souls had taken place and I knew then that we would see a lot of one another in the future. After talking with Dave and Erica I decided that I would make a point of holidaying in The Bahamas and visit them on their home ground as Dave had said that no one had ever visited them from the UK. The next day was spent sightseeing around Carlow before finally setting off for Dublin and the return journey to Holyhead. On the boat Geraldine and I had several conversations on the internet and we agreed to keep in touch with each other.

Well my friend as the months past we have been enjoying each other's company and now have strong feelings for each other. At first I had strong feelings of guilt, however on one of Pat's connections with me she assured me I was fine to do what I was doing and she would be waiting for me when I crossover. I mention this because so many people who grieve for a loved one find great difficulty in moving forward with their lives. Moving on does not mean forgetting or disrespecting your loved one for they are now living on a different dimension to us and although they can visit us from time to time they cannot come back to us as they were. But even so they still have the memories just like us that they have left behind. I do concede lots of people will have difficulty understanding this because of their emotional state which is part of their human-nous and of course if Pat was still on the earth plane none of this, Geraldine, the books, or my spiritual journey would probably ever have begun and you certainly would not be reading this catalogue of my journey.

I have visited various places of outstanding beauty in Carlow, Tullow and the surrounding area. For instance Altamont Gardens, Ballon, Co Carlow a beautiful period house set in the most wonderful gardens. The colours at varying times of the year are amazing. There is also Rathwood Garden Centre at Rath, Tullow, Co Carlow. A beautiful garden experience with plenty for children to do, or the Arboretum at Leighlinbridge, Co Carlow which has absolutely fantastic gardens set out with hand forged metal sculptures, lots of vivid colours and many other facilities. Again the Delta Sensory Gardens at Strawhall, Carlow beautifully structured gardens done in various themes and so peaceful. A little bit further south is Kilkenny with its magnificent castle and ancient town. However the one that stands out for me is The Rathgall Rath gealor the Ring of Ra near Shillelagh in County Wicklow. This is a Bronze Age hill fort dating from 1200- to 800BC and apart from being a place of beauty the Energy there is quite phenomenal. While I was there a friend from England rang me wanting some information, I told him I would text him when we left the hill fort and I got back to the car. Well I tried to text him but the letters were going across the screen so fast I couldn't stop them I wasn't even touching the phone, I eventually switched the phone off and I noticed my wrist watch had also stopped, all very strange indeed.

(Altamont Gardens, Ballon, Co Carlow)

(Rathwood Garden Centre at Rath, Tullow, Co Carlow)

(Delta Sensory Gardens at Strawhall, Carlow)

(Kilkenny Castle)

(The Rathgall Rath gealor the Ring of Ra near Shillelagh in County Wicklow)

I would like to mention at this point the special gifts my new found love Geraldine has; she has a great sense for telepathy and is able to manifest herself in different places. An example of this was one afternoon I was sat in my lounge at home when she appeared in the room and walked over to me and kissed me. Now I have had similar experiences before but it was quite eerie, though I must admit I enjoyed the moment and I hope she stays in my life for a long time to come. Talking about energy many other strange activities began to happen, I've spoken about orbs in my bedroom before but this is different, they are not orbs but large pieces of energy sometimes gold in colour but usually dark and dense. After my first experience of these phenomena I started to take hold of them in my hand and found I had the most weird sensation of heat travelling up my arms and into my body. I also noticed that if I put my hand into the energy my hand disappeared within it. On larger energies I have put my whole arm in and that to disappeared and reappeared as I withdrew from the energy. I have wondered what would happen if one was so large that I could walk into it would I come out the other side or perhaps find myself in another dimension. My friend you may find this all very hard to believe but I can only relate to you what happened as I experienced it.

Coming towards the end of 2016 I made several visits to the Midlands staying at the home of my friends Mac and Margaret. I have known them for about ten years during which time Mac and I had become very close friends; we were more like brothers. Right from the beginning of my journey I have talked to him about all of my experiences and he has always said "I'm not saying it never happened but unless I see with my own eyes I cannot believe it", please remember this if you will my friend as that statement will become very pertinent shortly. To put you further in the picture Mac is also the designer of the covers on my *Granddad You Have a Message* books and has in fact designed the cover of this book that you are currently reading. Well three weekends before Christmas I was staying with them and I noticed how gaunt he looked and I realised he had lost a lot of weight. When I mentioned this to him he said he didn't feel well and was in considerable pain. Normally on my visit I would take them out to dinner, but this time he asked if I would take Margaret as he did not feel up to it, this in itself I found strange as Mac enjoyed these nights out for the food and the banter. On the Sunday before I left to go home I suggested a visit to his Doctor was long overdue. In the past two years he had had Bowel Cancer and a Triple Heart by-pass and I felt all of these things were beginning to take their toll on him.

On the Monday morning Mac was taken into hospital and was told he only had a few weeks to live as his body was riddled with cancer. I must say this all came as a shock for all of us, I knew he was ill but I just didn't realise how ill. Well things went from bad to worse and he was given hours to live. During that night I had a vision of him stood by my bed, he told me how much he loved Geraldine and myself and how he would look after all his family as he loved them all so much. I noted the time; it was 04-55 am. Later that morning I was doing my daily walk along Newry beach when Margaret rang to say he had passed away at 05-30am, half an hour after he spoke with me, so his spirit had left his body shortly before he passed over.

That evening I was at my spiritual meeting and as I walked into the room I knew he was there as a corner of the room where the healing table is, was filled with brilliant white light. The medium for the service that night was Heddwen Lloyd Williams she came straight toward me and said a man who looked a bit like me was holding her very tight showing her his pain, she had to tell him she understood but to stop as it was hurting her. She came to me and said he was pointing to me saying that everything I had discussed with him in the past was exactly as I had described it. He went on to say how much he loved Margaret and his family and that he would look out for them. Well my friend, I was elated but Heddwen and the others could hardly believe that he had only passed that very morning. When I got into bed that night the room filled with the smell of cannabis and I knew he was still with me for he never went to bed without having a smoke of the stuff, I also had terrible chest pain and I realised he was showing me how painful it had been for him, I asked him to stop and once again I was free of pain. The next day I was driving to the Midlands to see his family and he was blowing in my face, I had to ask him to stop as it was distracting me. Talking to Geraldine that day she told me Mac had telepathically had a conversation with her and once again he reiterated how much he loved us all and that he would look after all of us. This episode has been a very moving loving experience for his family, Geraldine and of course myself. I would just add that on the day of his funeral the area of the room where his coffin stood was bathed in beautiful white light, Geraldine also witnessed this and we both knew that he was there with us all. Also I think the fact the music from the final song kept stopping and starting got everyone in the room realising he was there, he was a very special character who used to say "do not believe what I say go and research it for yourselves" and as I have said before: strange things happen when someone dies.

(Mac Goldie - my good friend)

It is my belief that when we pass on we our soul or spirit moves onto a different dimension leaving the now redundant human body behind to be dispensed of. Some might say but no one comes back to tell us what it's like.

Well I would dispute that statement based on my own experiences over the past six years. As I have said before you do not have to take my word for it, do your own research though I do believe many of you reading this will have already found out for yourselves.

Inspirational People or Angels?

In recent years I have been privileged to know some very inspirational people. My wife Pat, there was few people who came to see her when she was ill who didn't leave there a lot happier than when they walked through the door, her courage inspired many.

My friend Tom Attwater who has only been in my life for a short while, who has put all of his health problems to the back of his mind to raise funds for his little girl Kelli who has a childhood cancer. He has a brain tumour and has known for some time that the prognosis wasn't good, never the less he has put everything   before himself to make sure the Kelli Smith Fund hit its target of £500,000. Tom you are an inspiration to everyone who knows you and many others as well.

Then there is Tracey Hill a lady I met recently when I delivered to her a copy of my book. She showed me into her lounge and it was immediately obvious that she is very ill with breast cancer (reminded me a lot of Pat in her darkest days), however this lady was so upbeat and positive about her situation. She knows she is going to pass over but she is at one with this because she has absolute faith in the after-life. Her concerns are for her family and how they will cope with her passing. Concern for everyone but herself, I walked out of her flat after staying for two hours totally inspired and in awe of her courage. A courage based on the belief that her soul will continue to exist long after she sheds her earthly attire.

Apart from being inspirational beings they all have one other thing in common and that is that they are Angels. Pat in the afterlife and Tom and Tracey here on earth. (Both Tom and Tracy have since passed to The World of Spirit).

For me these three people have inspired me throughout 2014/15.

WHO, inspired you?

Of course these are three people there are many more in the world some will come and give to you others will receive from you. The thing is you will get no prior warning of their coming and how you react to them will determine how far you have progressed on your journey.

I think at this time this is the moment to bring to a close to the story it has been a long journey from the dark into the light a road that has seen me in the main through the most horrible thing that affects us all at some time in our lives. I thank you my friend for your company and patience and hope and pray that if you should find yourself in this situation journeying through my experience with me will help you.

Love and Light and God bless you all.